Re-Structuring the Government of New York City

Edward N. Costikyan
Maxwell Lehman

The Praeger Special Studies program—utilizing the most modern and efficient book production techniques and a selective worldwide distribution network—makes available to the academic, government, and business communities significant, timely research in U.S. and international economic, social, and political development.

Re-Structuring the Government of New York City

Report of
the Scott Commission
Task Force on
Jurisdiction and Structure

PRAEGER SPECIAL STUDIES IN U.S. ECONOMIC, SOCIAL, AND POLITICAL ISSUES

Praeger Publishers   New York   Washington   London

PRAEGER PUBLISHERS
111 Fourth Avenue, New York, N.Y. 10003, U.S.A.
5, Cromwell Place, London S.W.7, England

Published in the United States of America in 1972
by Praeger Publishers, Inc.

Library of Congress Catalog Card Number: 72-86838

Printed in the United States of America

This report was prepared for The Temporary Commission to Make
a Study of the Governmental Operations of the City of New York
by the Task Force on Jurisdiction and Structure, directed by
Edward N. Costikyan and Maxwell Lehman, and was submitted on
March 15, 1972. The Appendix, "Effects of Re-Structure on
Federal Programs in New York City," was submitted to the
commission on April 24, 1972, as a supplement to the report.

This is our plan for a new kind of New York City. Our objectives have been to develop the model for a governmental system in which, within the framework of a strong central City government, there may once again be local communities in New York City with which people identify; in which residents may take part and know their participation is meaningful; and in which the day-to-day services may be better delivered.

We know that re-structuring will not be the panacea for all the urban ills that beset the City; nor do we present it as a total solution. This report is not an academic exercise in unrealizable expectations. We indicate what re-structuring cannot do, as well as what may be obtained from it.

The processes by which we reached our conclusions are visible in this book. We made certain assumptions and adopted certain premises; we state what they are. We have rejected certain formulations; we indicate why. We have put together instruments of government in new ways; we explain how those would operate. We have recognized that there are various ways to set up local governments; we examine many of them. In addition, we have listened to New Yorkers in all five boroughs, we have studied other cities comparable to New York in population and geography, and we have read the literature.

Our proposal has been designed specifically to fit the special requirements of New York City, with its varied population groups, its unique and complex history, and its great cultural, social, economic, and spatial diversity. We have been sensitive to the necessity of retaining a "whole" city, and our plan contains checks and balances to prevent fragmentation. We have opted for the strong-mayor form of local government, and find this to be feasible within a frame that includes numerous "small towns."

The work process has been much like fitting pieces of a puzzle together. We have tried to make the parts of the structure fit neatly, each with the other.

We were warned that the cost of re-structuring would be prohibitive, and this was a real concern. But just the opposite is true: the design we suggest will not be more expensive than the present system of government; it may be less so.

We have learned from other re-structures, those that went smoothly and those that went badly. And we know the importance of flexibility and time. The new structure must be carefully built. The new districts must have the opportunity to proceed at their own pace. There must be provision for a learning period, as well as for continuous change. The transition must be judiciously, delicately, and intelligently handled, with full understanding of the many interests involved.

This study is not meant to be confined narrowly to consideration of city government. Rather, we conceive of it as part of a broader concept—one that encompasses the need to reexamine the U.S. federal system of government and the relationships among local, State, regional, and Federal governments, and to determine—in light of technological changes, recent history, migrations, and new burdens of government—what new arrangements are required.

The members of the State Study Commission for New York City have never been remote from us. They have given us their time, shared with us their own special knowledge, sat through long (but intensely interesting) days of public hearings, read vast quantities of literature on the subject. Our thanks go to the commission's chairman, Stuart N. Scott; to its members, Shirley Chisholm, Lucius D. Clay, Herman Kahn, and Robert J. Milano; and to its energetic executive director, Stephen Berger.

The staff people who worked on this project are an unusually able group. It was they who often put us back on the right track when we went off on some "far-out" idea. Without them, this report would be less than it is. The group consisted of Walter G. Farr, Jr., professor of law at the Vanderbilt Law School, New York University, who has written a soon-to-be-published book on the subject of decentralization in New York; Jeffrey Wood, who also worked on that project; Dr. Joseph Rappaport, of Fordham University, who prepared special reports dealing with service allocations; Kathy Imholz, who supplied us with careful legal analysis and helped us absorb the literature on decentralization; W. Bernard Richland, our principal advisor on the legal problems implicit in our proposal; James L. Garnett and Anna H. Clark, our indefatigable researchers, who never counted hours of work and never hesitated to tell us when they disagreed with any of our conclusions; and Cristina Kazan who, as administrative aide, pulled everything together in a most efficient manner.

In addition, there was Edward J. Logue, who, while not formally a member of the Task Force, made continuing and invaluable contributions to our analysis and to our understanding of the problems of urban government.

But the total result of this undertaking is ours, and the responsibility for it is ours alone.

Task Force on Jurisdiction and Structure

Edward N. Costikyan, Chairman
Maxwell Lehman, Vice Chairman

CONTENTS

LIST OF FIGURES

Re-Structuring the Government of New York City

1

INTRODUCTION:
A PROPOSED NEW STRUCTURE
OF CITY GOVERNMENT

Descriptions of governmental structure frequently start with a summary of the functions of the chief governmental official—the king, president, governor, or mayor. The citizen appears on the chart, if at all, only as an unimportant cipher at the bottom. However, such an analysis unconsciously produces a subtle distortion of the governmental process. It emphasizes the role and significance of the public official and diminishes the significance of the citizen and voter. More significantly, it presupposes a hierarchical relationship in government with a man "at the top" in whom all lines of authority find their terminus and on whom all governmental jurisdictions converge. Therefore, one of the central questions that needs to be addressed is: to what extent is this traditional analytic approach appropriate for New York City in the last portion of the twentieth century?

In our view, a critical element in any effective reorganization of the City's governmental structure is the recognition that there is a far more important role to be played by the citizen. This inevitably means rethinking the conventional concept that everything must be centralized at the top of some pyramidal structure.

THREE BASIC CONSIDERATIONS

The Citizen and Government

The top of the structure proposed by the Task Force is the voter, who has three significant governmental roles. First, he is the source of all the governmental power exercised by public officials. Second, he is the recipient of governmental services and the subject of such restraints as society imposes. Third, he is a governing force himself, ideally exercising some degree of quasi-governmental responsibility in his community.

Persuading each person to take on the third of these roles is essential if nearly 8 million people are to live together successfully in a city such as New York. Most New Yorkers are not performing the role adequately under the city's present structure, which, implicitly or explicitly, requires government to solve all the problems its citizens create—even those problems that result from the people's own inattention, negligence, or disdain for the City's environment.

There are, of course, considerable differences from city to city in the attitudes that people display toward their local government, their fellow residents, and their community environment. The environment tends to reflect the attitude. In some cities, for example, the streets are cleaner than in New York. This is partly because the people in those cities are sufficiently self-disciplined so that they do not throw trash on the streets as frequently as New Yorkers do, expecting the City to pick it up and complaining that it is not picked up rapidly enough.

Is Copenhagen safer than New York? One reason for this is the self-discipline of Danish citizens. Similarly, Stockholm's schools, transit system and public buildings are largely free of the kinds of vandalism that cost New Yorkers millions of dollars each year. This can be attributed partly to the fact that Swedes do not regard public property as fair game for destruction, as so many New Yorkers do without fear of societal disapproval, let alone legal sanctions.

No structure of municipal government can, by itself, induce a citizen suddenly to become more responsible for his own actions. The citizen's self-discipline found in Copenhagen, Stockholm, and other cities is substantially the result of lengthy and complex cultural and socialization processes. However, adoption of a sound governmental mechanism—the kind New York City currently lacks—can facilitate and encourage the redevelopment of a sense of local pride and local responsibility, as well as make it easier for the city to establish standards for its residents to meet. An improved structure can make people understand that government is a tool to be used instead of a remote establishment to be blamed. Furthermore, it can remind the citizen of his proper role—as a responsible participant in the governing process, not merely an occasional recipient of government largess.

The Delegation of Power

A corollary to the principle that the citizen is the source of all governmental power exercised by public officials is that the citizen

should grant that power to government officials only to the extent necessary to produce effective and efficient government. The extent of
necessary delegation varies according to the governmental function to
be performed. Because one function—foreign affairs, for example—is
properly vested in the President of the United States, it does not follow
that each and every function—street cleaning, for example—should
likewise be subject to the control of the same public official.

Although this distinction appears to be all too obvious, it is
actually ignored in New York City's present governmental structure,
wherein all functions are vested in the central City government.

It is clear that each governmental function should rationally be
assigned to the level of government that can best perform it. In such
a formulation, a corollary is that aspects of a governmental function
may be allocated to different governmental levels. For example, one
level may provide funding, a second level may set standards, and a
third level may be charged with service delivery.

The question arises as to which level to select if two levels are
apparently equally capable of performing a particular function. We
have resolved that question in accordance with the principle: The
closer governmental authority is to the source of power—the citizen—
the better. Government physically and psychologically remote from
the citizen tends to be less visible, less accountable, less responsive.
Distant delegation of authority should be made only when the nature of
the function to be performed requires it.

Bearing in mind these concepts of power delegation, we can
look at New York City's existing structure and find a tremendous gap
between the citizen and the executive authority to whom responsibility
has been entrusted. Unlike any other city in the world comparable in
population and geography, New York City attempts to govern itself
with a single level of City-wide executive government responsible for
the well-being of nearly 8 million people residing in an area covering
320 square miles. The remoteness of government from the citizen
who is the source of its power and the recipient of its services has,
in recent years, been the cause of increasing dissatisfaction. In the
Forest Hills housing confrontation, for example, it has gone beyond
dissatisfaction to something approaching local anarchy.

After more than half a century of centralization, New York has
achieved what generations of reformers and theoreticians have sought—
a strong-mayor form of government, with all lines of executive
authority, including budgetary authority, terminating at the top of the
pyramid. And the citizen, at the bottom, feels excluded from the
governmental process.

Centralization versus Localization

As even its proponents increasingly concede, centralization has not proven the answer to governmental inefficiency. Several other solutions have been suggested. One of them consists of further centralization. We find this unacceptable for a host of reasons, the most practical being that the voters will not buy more of the same medicine that has already made their body politic so ill.

Another proposed solution is to keep the centralized structure but superimpose a veneer of localism upon it. One version of this solution involves creating another centralized structure with local offices (representing the central government) in various locations throughout the City. We find this solution unacceptable (as we do all others that fail to delegate both power and accountability to local levels), because it deals with cosmetics, not substance; it involves wholly unnecessary and costly duplication of government staff, vests no real power in the local offices, and makes no place for the local citizen.

Another solution is sometimes suggested, usually at election time: elect a new mayor and he will make City government work. But the shortcomings of City government with which we are concerned are more fundamental. They cannot be cured merely by changing the man at the top.

The remaining alternative (other than doing nothing and hoping for the best), and the alternative this Task Force recommends, is the one every major world-city of New York's size and status has adopted: that is to allocate certain governmental services to small units of government more capable of performing those services, while at the same time retaining a strong central government to perform the functions that require sizable resources and coordinated effort. City problems spilling over into other parts of the metropolitan region should be dealt with regionally.

Under the Task Force's proposal, each local entity within the city would have a population sufficient to achieve reasonable efficiency in the performance of those functions vested in it, but not so large as to suffer the disabilities of remoteness and inefficiency that characterize present City government.

OPERATING GUIDELINES OF
THE TASK FORCE

A set of premises, guidelines, and value judgments emerged as we proceeded with our task. These were:

—The people of New York City can be trusted to govern them-selves. The more of them we bring effectively into democratic society, the stronger that society will be. Mistakes will be made as residents learn the art and science of governance. This is an acceptable risk.

—Local districts can be established without fragmenting the City. The reverse is likely: The City of New York will be strengthened by the intimate involvement of local people in their local affairs, while matters of City-wide concern are handled on a City-wide level. It is feasible to work out a mix of services, assigning them on a logical basis to those governmental units that can most effectively deliver them.

—A two-level service-delivery structure of municipal government requires a mechanism to mediate between them and to guide realloca-tion of services between the levels.

—Flexibility must be built into the plan, thereby allowing local units to develop at their own pace and with enough managerial and financial support to be viable within the total framework.

—Insofar as possible, existing structures should be used in re-structuring the government.

—Existing civil service personnel must form the human building blocks of the restructured system.

—Various problems spill over City borders and should be dealt with regionally. Localization and regionalization must proceed, but decentralization of services need not wait until an acceptable plan of regionalization is developed.

A PRELIMINARY NOTE ON THE
MAYORALTY, FRAGMENTA-
TION, BUDGET, AND CITIZEN
PARTICIPATION

Many people who have not seen this report have expressed fears that it calls for stripping the mayor's office of its powers, fragment-ing the City, and adding large sums to the City budget for local dis-tricts; some people also maintain that citizen participation in local governments would be low. These fears, though, are unwarranted. Let us consider each of them briefly:

—In our formulation, the mayorality remains a strong office, possibly stronger than it is today. The mayor is relieved of respon-sibility for functions that he should not and cannot reasonably perform. He would thus be allowed to devote his energies to policy and program planning for the City as a whole.

—As to charges that re-structuring would fragment the City, the City is already fragmented today. The proposed structure is designed to link together the various segments and communities of the City with the central City government more intimately than ever before. The Task Force has designed an inter-relationship with connections and checks and balances at all points, thereby permitting the citizen's voice to be heard effectively and the central government to operate more sensitively than it does now.

—The cost of the proposed new structure has been tentatively computed. Far from even approaching the figures mentioned, it will not exceed $30 million, which is three-tenths of one percent of the City's total annual budget.

For a representative local district, cost estimates for parttime local councilmen, local executive and staff, operating expenses, and new space would amount to less than $700,000 in new expenditures. This is a miniscule amount when compared to the total City budget. Even if the annual costs of each district were as much as $1 million— an increase to provide for presently unforeseen needs, such as a planning study, an important social service analysis, even a major augmentation of present management resources—an annual expenditure of $30 million in 30 districts to enhance the quality of local government would still be dwarfed by the cost of the present highly centralized administration. And since the city's superagencies would have no place in the proposed system, there would be a corresponding reduction in costs, with the likelihood of a probable saving on the bottom line (the central executive management programs alone of the present superagencies exceed the projected costs of all the new districts).

As for the line agencies, when they devolve from the central to the local tier, their budgets would devolve with them. Most of the new positions can and should be filled by existing personnel and within existing budgetary allocations. Under our plan, therefore, it would cost no more to take a chest X ray locally than it now costs to take it centrally. There is even reason to believe that elements of lower cost may be foreseen, in that local visibility of public employees can have a positive impact on productivity. (A fuller discussion of cost elements appears in Chapter 6, in the section entitled "The Transition.")

—We do not accept the idea that local residents would not participate in a re-structured system. We argue the reverse: Grant to the local resident a sense that he has a voice in local matters affecting him, and you have created an incentive to participate. If a system of elective local governments with good local communication is set up, then there will soon be an incentive to political parties to "get the vote out"—and that means citizen participation; in cities comparable in size to that envisioned for each of the local districts, up to 75 percent of the registered voters participate in local elections.

WHAT RE-STRUCTURING CAN
AND CANNOT DO

The re-structuring of New York City's government is a matter
of enormous consequence, so it has to be approached realistically.
This means, among other things, recognizing what re-structuring can
and cannot do.

—Re-structuring will not solve the desperate problem of street
crime. But it can provide for a more intimate relationship between
local residents and police, and facilitate citizen-police cooperation.
It will establish local governments with strong motivation to mount
neighborhood attacks on the narcotics problem. And local districts
are much more capable than a central City Hall of dealing with local
conditions that breed crime.

—Re-structuring will not increase the City's housing supply.
But by devolving housing code enforcement and inspection to local
governments, it is probable that much housing deterioration may be
halted. And by giving the district governments responsibility for
housing management and maintenance, these functions can almost
certainly be better performed. Moreover, decentralization spurs
increased pride in community, which in turn can well have affirmative
"spillover" effects on the local housing situation.

—Re-structuring will not assure increased revenues to meet
the City's needs. But local councils can be given the tools to monitor
closely how funds are being spent in their neighborhoods and to determine local priorities. And the establishment of viable "small
towns" would tend to improve and enrich local areas; one spin-off
of such an arrangement might be a strengthened economic base. (In
addition, a supplemental study by this Task Force indicates that
Federal funds currently received by the city would not be reduced as
a result of re-structuring.)

—Re-structuring will not solve the enormous problems of
poverty in New York City. But under it, much more personalized
attention can be provided to welfare recipients. If income maintenance
financing is taken over by the Federal government (as, in our opinion,
it should be), the delivery of social services by the local district
governments would be more humane than under the present degrading
system.

—Re-structuring will not solve the City's budgetary problems.
But such a change would make it necessary to analyze the City's
budgetary needs in terms of the functions to be performed. And, as
functions are broken down into their components, it would also
necessitate reanalysis of existing budgets to determine what is really
needed and what is merely budgetary inertia. And it offers the

possibility that local districts would be able to secure a higher level
of productivity than the present remote centralized administrations
if administering functions are basically local.
    —Re-structuring is not a cure-all. It is one way to deal with
the frustrations, the irritations, the alienation of citizens. It is one
way to deal with the remoteness and inaccessibility of government; it
is a way to overcome the jumble of service delivery lines in the City,
along with increasingly poor service delivery; and to break into the
many-layered government and give some openings to the citizen who
desires contact with his government. It is a way to give the local
citizen a stronger voice in matters that concern his daily life. It is
a way to provide a number of small communities in the City with the
amenities, pleasures and sense of identity characteristic of small-
town life. It is a way for mobilizing community energies constructively
through built-in institutional mechanisms, thereby allowing citizens
to initiate and to propose, rather than merely to react and to veto.
It is a way to humanize service delivery, and that by itself means
making it better. It is a way to enlarge democratic society by bringing
more people, now estranged from it, into effective participation—and
thus, incidentally, opening a new reservoir of human talent for the
common good.

FORMS OF DECENTRALIZATION

    "Decentralization" may take any one of several forms:
    —Decentralization involving the delivery of certain services to
local areas, with control remaining at the top level and local civil
servants carrying out the mandates of their superiors. This form,
known as administrative decentralization, does not differ greatly from
the traditional field services of municipal departments.
    —Decentralization based on an effort to coordinate services more
effectively within local neighborhoods, so that employees of municipal
departments who work within designated areas act together on common
problems. This is a variant form of administrative decentralization,
sometimes called territorial decentralization, close to the plan an-
nounced in January 1972 by the New York City government. In this
plan, though, local residents have no legally mandated voice in local
matters affecting their destinies.
    —A third form of decentralization, designed to involve the com-
munity in certain designated programs. Examples are local poverty
councils and community corporations. But evidence to date demonstrates that local residents do not participate; voting is often as low
as five percent. The reasons are that many local residents do not
know what is going on, and those who are informed come to recognize

that they do not exercise real power, that basic decisions are still made elsewhere, and that the various local organizations have not been effective.

—A fourth form of decentralization involving the devolution of services to local areas, with funds allocated to locally elected groups for the purpose of sustaining those functions. Ultimate control under this system nevertheless still rests with the higher levels of government. This is a mild form of political decentralization.

—A fifth form of decentralization involving local councils, partly elected and partly appointed, with services partially supervised locally, but ultimately controlled by the mayor. The plan contains elements of duplication and overlapping.

Although it is possible to work out permutations and combinations of these various forms of decentralization, they all have in common the failure to grant to the local communities three strengths: independent, locally elected councils; control of local service delivery; and budget-making power.

An interesting concept has been suggested by Professor Peter Eisinger of the University of Wisconsin. He refers to the principle of control-sharing, which takes two main forms. "One may be called decentralization, a form of organization designed to share control through the transfer of some policy-making authority to residents of particular neighborhood territories. The second may be called client representation, a scheme for sharing control by institutionalizing representation of client groups on bodies vested with policy-making powers over bureaucratic agencies."[1]

Models of decentralization with control remaining at the top governmental level are inevitably no more than variant forms of centralization, since the chain of command runs from the lower to the upper echelons where the real decision-making power continues to reside.

A plan of true decentralization must include clear differentiation between those functions allocated to the City-wide tier and those functions allocated to the local tier, with local participation on an elected basis. Only in this way can duplication be avoided and effective decision-making and operating strength be placed in the hands of the local community.

It is important, however, to avoid substituting the whim of a lay body in a professional or technical area for professional knowledge and expertise; the service of professionals is essential in a complex society.

WHAT THE TASK FORCE PROPOSES

The Task Force on Jurisdiction and Structure has developed a new structure for the government of New York City. It has been designed to satisfy two basic needs: (1) providing improved delivery of services, and (2) making government more sensitive, more accountable, and more accessible to the city's residents. This proposed structure includes:

—a strong mayoralty and a central level of City-wide services;

—local elected governing districts with sufficient authority and budget to carry out a variety of local functions;

—allocation of functions on a rational basis, placing each service at the level of government where it logically belongs in terms of service delivery;

—governmental machinery to make the system work.

The Proposed Structure
consists of

A number of elected local governmental units, for delivery of local services	—and—	One central government, headed by the mayor and elected City-wide, for delivery of central services

and

A central governing authority with
ultimate jurisdiction over both,
consisting of

The City Policy Board, headed by the mayor	—and—	A City Council, made up of representatives of the local districts

The 12 essential elements of the proposed structure are as follows:

1. Delineation of local service-delivery districts, to be legally designated as governing and operating governmental units; plus retention of a central service-delivery sector for those services that are designated as central.

2. Establishment of a local council in each district, elected from geographic subdivisions of the district.

3. Election or appointment in each district of a local executive officer in charge of day-to-day service delivery.

4. Retention by the central City government of budgetary powers over functions allocated to it; a grant of financial and budgetary powers to the local districts; a scheme of resource allocation between the two levels.

5. Reallocation of services among the levels of government, in such a manner that each level performs those functions it is best equipped to perform; reallocation is based on understanding that the tiers of government are not "higher" and "lower"—only different.

6. Creation of a system of controls, whereby a local district that fails to perform its services properly would be temporarily superseded.

7. Reorganization of the Board of Estimate into the City Policy Board, which would become the major policy-making unit of the central government and the mediating vehicle for inter-district and district-central matters. The Policy Board would be equipped with governmental tools to perform its tasks effectively.

8. Retention of the City Council as the central legislative body, its members being elected from districts correlated with the new local districts, if possible (see discussion of local districts in Chapter 3). The council would have certain review powers over the central City agencies.

9. Retention of the mayor as chief executive officer of the central government; as presiding member of the City Policy Board, with a weighted vote; and as major spokesman for the whole City.

10. Retention of the comptroller as chief auditing officer, both of the central and of the local governments.

11. Retention of the borough presidents, renaming them county executives and vesting in them substantial supervisory powers as members of the City Policy Board.

12. Establishment of instruments to facilitate citizen-government communication.

THE BASIC REASONS FOR
RE-STRUCTURING

Our analysis starts with three observations:

—Of the major world cities comparable in population and complexity, only New York attempts to govern itself with a single level of government.

—There is immense dissatisfaction among New Yorkers with the City's delivery of ordinary local government services.

—Government in New York City has become increasingly remote; the City's residents increasingly demand a form of government closer to them and to which they can relate more directly.

FIGURE 1

Proposed Structure of New York City
Central Government and Local Governments

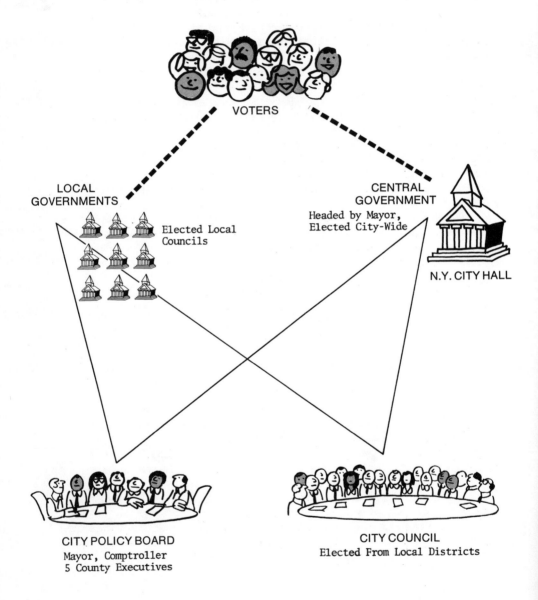

Other World Cities

Amid all the comments about the dismal conditions in New York (and in other U.S. cities as well), no one suggests that the government of Paris, of Berlin, of Hamburg, of Tokyo, of Moscow, or of London is falling apart. The reason is simply that none of those foreign cities is falling apart. Although they have differing governmental organizations, each of them has a two-level structure, with local functions administered locally on one level of government and central functions delivered centrally by another level of government, each with large areas of independence from the other.[2]

In contrast, New York City is widely regarded as a municipality in crisis. There are many causes. One of them is the City's many-layered, highly centralized, single-level governmental structure.

From this it does not follow that New York City can simply borrow the Paris or Berlin or London or Moscow governmental structure. It does follow, however, that there should be serious analysis of the way those governments work, and of the desirability of some form of two-level government in New York City.

The Task Force having made that analysis, it recommends the adoption of a two-level structure for New York City. Its proposed plan, though, is not based upon the form used in any particular European or U.S. city, but rather on New York's own unique characteristics, political history, and heterogeneous population, as well as on lessons learned from study of governments of other major world cities. The result of the Task Force's work, therefore, is not a borrowed structure but one specifically designed for New York City and its pressing governmental problems.

Service Delivery

The delivery of municipal services has deteriorated in New York City. This deterioration has been a factor in the exodus of middle-class residents; it has also adversely affected the City's economy and the life-styles of its residents. The demand for stemming the deterioration of services has led to a search for new approaches, including better delivery of municipal services in local communities. The reason for this search is that New York City's present structure is incapable of delivering local services efficiently and effectively.

The hierarchies of the City departments that direct the delivery of local services are too large and cumbersome to permit effective management of such basic functions as street cleaning, street repairs, housing code enforcement, local park maintenance, and personal health and social services.

The citizen's problem in securing services is complicated by the fact that New York City's governmental service-delivery districts are not rationally coordinated or related. Sanitation districts, mental health districts, health districts, police precincts, community planning districts, school districts, Model City neighborhoods, OEO-designated poverty areas, are all different. There are no local centers to bring their work into alignment, to relate them to the neighborhoods, or to make it easy for a citizen to obtain the services he needs.

The various district lines overlap in enormous profusion. They have grown historically, each department creating such district lines as it felt were useful, quite oblivious of other possibly competing district lines. As a result, the delivery of local services by various municipal departments is largely unrelated to the delivery of other services by other departments. There is little joint use of facilities and staff, no development of joint statistical services. There is a noticeable lack of governmental effort, either to consolidate closely related functions or to eliminate program duplication. In fact, the proliferation of districts renders invisible both the present overlapping and any possible future economies. The separate agencies are, in effect, separate, single-purpose governments, each going its own way.

The result is fragmented and ineffective municipal government. As Edward J. Logue pointed out in his testimony to this Task Force: "Anybody who has had any operating governmental experience at any level, any community leader who has attempted to preserve or improve his neighborhood knows that working with just one department or one governmental function is not enough. Keeping the streets clean is related to housing inspection, which is related to public health, which is related to fire and police. . . ."

OVERLAPPING DISTRICT LINES

The delivery of local services by municipal departments is largely unrelated to the delivery of other services by other departments. There are sanitation districts, health districts, political districts, planning districts, school districts, Model City neighborhoods, and OEO-designated poverty areas. The lines overlap in enormous profusion. There is no central place in the community where the citizens can go for service or information. Figures 2 through 7 follow, showing various district lines in the borough of Brooklyn. Figure 7 puts the lines of five districts together, demonstrating how unrelated they are.   ⟶

FIGURE 2

Mental Health Areas in Brooklyn

FIGURE 3

Police Districts in Brooklyn

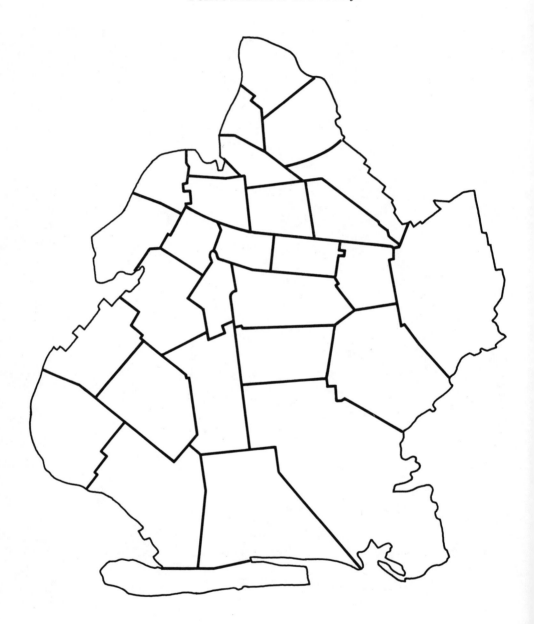

FIGURE 4

Health Districts in Brooklyn

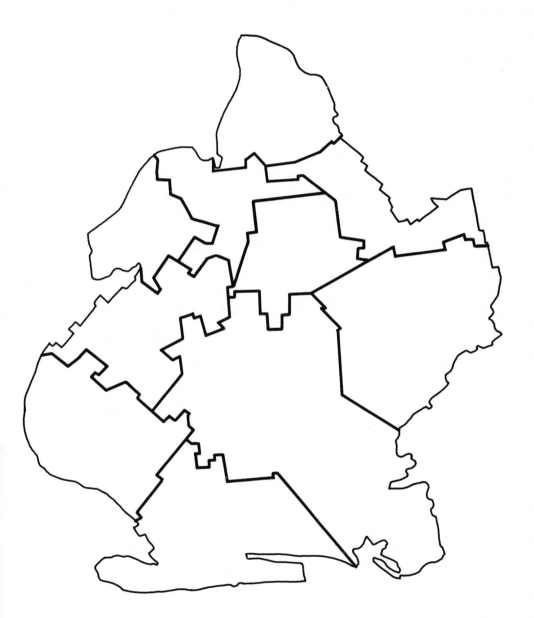

FIGURE 5

Planning Districts in Brooklyn

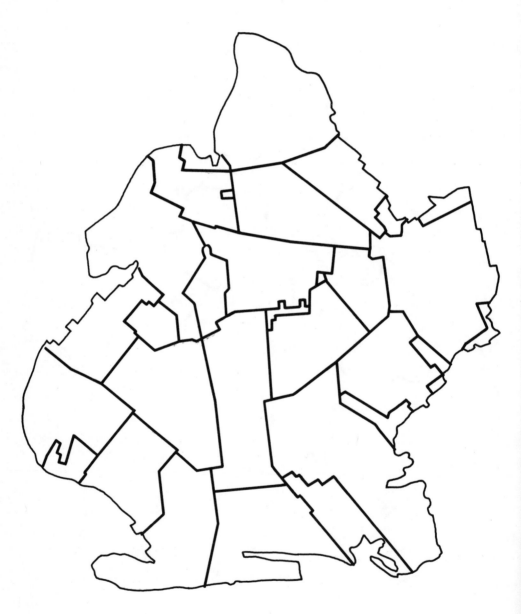

FIGURE 6

Community School Districts in Brooklyn

FIGURE 7

Boundaries of Five Different District Systems in Brooklyn

DISTRICT LINES SEEN TOGETHER

Remoteness of Government

    While the public demand for better service delivery has been increasing, there has also been a growing citizen insistence upon greater accessibility of the government to the people and greater participation by residents near the point of service delivery. Concentration of power in the executive branch of New York's single-tier municipal government has not made government more accessible to the City's residents. Rather, it has done the opposite; with increasing centralization, the organizational structure of municipal government has become more and more cumbersome, fragmented, and remote.

    In addition, the continued preoccupation of the City's highest officials with local service-delivery problems results in inadequate attention to strategic policy problems, as policy-makers and administrators get bogged down in day-to-day detail.

    Another major factor is that elected officials—including borough presidents, Congressmen, and State and City legislators—are spending inordinate amounts of time as quasi-ombudsmen and expediters on behalf of their constituents. Their activity in this area is principally an effort to stimulate the executive arm of government into taking the kinds of action it is already mandated to take. But in their efforts both to serve their constituents and to prod government into action, the elected officials often neglect their legislative duties; the legislative function obviously suffers as a result.

The Failure of Attempted Political Solutions

    If the City's governmental deficiencies were attributable merely to the incapacity of the present administration, as has been so often asserted (former administrations suffered the same charges), the solution would be simple: elect a new administration and leave the structure alone. But the problem is more fundamental. Since World War II, this City has had four different styles of municipal administration. Each started with great hope; each of the first three ended with citizen dissatisfaction, resulting in a new and different style of administration replacing the previous one.

    The O'Dwyer administration was substantially the last dominated by political machines and ended in citizen dissatisfaction. The Impelliteri administration reflected a revolt by the voters against the machines and purported to be "independent"; it, too, ended in citizen dissatisfaction. The Impelliteri regime was replaced by the Wagner administration, which represented the culmination of the search for managerial excellence; yet despite attainment of a high degree of

administrative quality, this also ended in citizen dissatisfaction. The
Wagner administration was succeeded by the Lindsay administration,
which asserted that it would initiate high-quality, nonpolitical public
administration. The problem of adequate service delivery still remains.

The Need for More Basic Solutions

None of these changes in political administration has dealt with
what the Task Force regards to be the basic problem. We believe that
what is needed is more fundamental than a change in administration.
Effective City government requires elimination of the structural
cause of governmental inertia.

One cause of this inertia is the centralized administration of
what are, by their nature, local services. For example, surely it
should not require approval of a high Sanitation Department official to
obtain a change in the location of a street-cleaning sign. Yet that
is the rule throughout the city,—except in five test areas established
on January 14, 1972, by the City's Office of Neighborhood Government.

What has been even more persuasive is the advice and counsel
the Task Force has received from many participants in New York
City's government, from observers and students of that government,
from numerous representatives of citizens' groups, and from private
citizens who addressed us in our public hearings. The consensus
with which they endorsed the concept of two-level government is even
more striking since almost all of them have reached their decision
not by looking at Europe, not by looking at other U.S. cities, but by
looking at the way in which New York City's own municipal government functions.

As for the people of New York City, they are frustrated, sometimes resigned, sometimes angry, often helpless, almost always dis-
satisfied. A remarkable unanimity of view—one that crosses political
party, economic, and class lines—demonstrates strong dissatisfaction
with service delivery in the City and a powerful—perhaps irresistible—
desire by the people to exercise greater control over decisions
affecting their destinies. This desire is evidenced by a proliferation
of citizen organizations of all kinds—civic groups, community organizations, neighborhood clubs, semipolitical groups—that attempt by
such tools as they can devise to have some "voice" in what happens
to them. The public hearings of the Task Force on Jurisdiction and
Structure have demonstrated one significant result of this proliferation: an increasing citizen sophistication about the instruments of
governmental power and a growing public assurance that these instruments can be better wielded at the local level than they now are
centrally.

2

CRITERIA FOR
REALLOCATION
OF SERVICES

The Task Force has attempted to establish certain criteria in determining the allocation of public services for the City's residents under a re-structured system of municipal government.[3] These criteria are:

—Power may be shared by various units of government, i.e., funding by one unit, setting of standards and codes by another, service delivery by a third. This principle has been central to the Task Force's deliberations concerning allocation of services.

—The lines of service delivery should be correlated with local district boundaries.*

—The unit of government delivering a service should have a geographic jurisdiction large enough for effective performance.

—The governmental unit performing a function should have the legal, fiscal, and administrative capability to carry out its assigned tasks.

—The governmental unit responsible for providing any service should be of a size compatible with the utilization of that service primarily within the jurisdiction.

—Decisions should be made at the lowest governmental level possible, thus assuring swiftest response.**

―――――――――

*Under this concept, those services delivered by the local districts are within its territorial jurisdiction. Central services, such as police precincts, would be correlated with the local district lines. However, such correlation is not practicable in a few instances, as in the case of fire and regional hospital complexes.

**The Task Force has considered but not accepted the recommendation that certain service-delivery obligations be delegated to the borough presidents.

—The governmental unit to which a service is assigned should be large enough to permit realization of economies of scale, wherever possible.

—Services should be assigned to the level of government that offers the best conditions and opportunities for active citizen participation while permitting adequate service-delivery performance.

—Certain services should be shared. Others, clearly regional, should eventually be assigned to a regional governmental entity.

—Quasi-governmental units, such as local poverty groups, community corporations, addiction service agencies, should be included within the jurisdiction of the local districts.

—Not every local district would require every possible service. On the other hand, two or more districts could undertake to perform a given service jointly. Or one district could contract with another or, indeed, with the private sector, in cases where that may appear more efficient.

The above criteria do not deal with two items of importance, each of which, though, does require a brief comment here.

The first is education. The Task Force has not dealt with this area, because recently-enacted State law has made major changes and a new educational approach has been activated. Nevertheless, we do suggest that, in a re-structured City government, the lines of education districts eventually be coordinated with those of the local districts.

The second item consists of the City's present super-agencies. As now constituted, these agencies would have no place in the proposed system. Moreover, it has become clear, in six years of experimentation, that delivery of services has not improved since the establishment of the super-agencies. Public hearings held by the Task Force revealed immense dissatisfaction with their performance. The super-agencies added yet another layer of government, downgraded City departments, and extended the bureaucratic ladder between citizens and decision makers. The Task Force recommends that the State Study Commission for New York City undertake an examination of these super-agencies.

SERVICE REALLOCATION: A SAMPLE

The process of reallocating functions to the central and local service districts requires a function-by-function analysis of every City government agency. Following is an example of service reallocation in a single agency, undertaken in line with the established criteria*

Central Government	Local Governments
Health research	Chest clinics
Control of communicable disease	Dental clinics
Statistics	Eye clinics
Rat control	Immunization
Health codes	Diabetes clinics
Standard setting	Poison control centers
	Social hygiene
	Child health
	Nutrition education
	Maternal and infant care
	Restaurant code enforcement
	Sanitary inspections
	Ambulatory health service facilities
	Laboratories

The rationale for these reallocations lies in the nature of the agency's functions. Health research must be carried on in the broadest way possible, utilizing resources of the entire City and receiving grants that would be available only for the larger entity. Neither epidemics nor rats pay attention to local borders. So the prediction and control of epidemics and rat populations must be a City-wide— even region- and State-wide activity. The attack on the rat population cannot halt at local district borders, but the local districts must also be expected to play their part in combatting both epidemics and rats. Furthermore, health codes need to be City-wide because the highest standards must prevail for the entire City; otherwise, standards could tend toward the lowest common denominator. On the other hand, the enforcement of health codes is a local function, best carried out in the smaller local areas where violations are more visible and inspections swifter. In addition, under the proposed formula, health services are better delivered locally, where the impersonality and coldness of big government are lessened.

----

*The example, though, does not include all the health services delivered by the City's public health agencies.

An interesting proposal for dealing with health and hospital services was enunciated in the Piel Report in 1969,[4] which indicates that such matters, although fraught with complexities, hodgepodge, and overlapping, could be quite rationally determined. The report proposes a concentric system of facilities. Community hospitals, caring for people with common, short-term medical problems, would service areas in the 200,000-300,000 population range (which would correspond to the local districts recommended herein). At still another level, for service populations of 30,000-50,000, would be units providing ambulatory services, preventive and remedial health services. Related to each community hospital would be a teaching hospital complex, serving much larger populations—in the vicinity of 1,500,000— and capable of treating the most complex medical conditions.

The hearings held by the Task Force on Jurisdiction and Structure indicate a strong desire for community hospitals under community control. The community hospitals could be transferred to the local district governments.

An additional advantage of developing outpatient clinics to the local districts relates to the increased possibilities of coordination among agencies. Local outpatient clinics could be tied in with local social service centers, which provide related services. So the local resident would not need to wend his way among a number of agencies and unrelated bureaucracies, often located far from each other, as he does now. Such a new arrangement would be a particular boon to the City's poor and elderly.

SERVICE AND FUNCTIONS: PRELIMINARY
REALLOCATION SAMPLE

The Task Force is now making a complete analysis of all functions and services. The following reallocation list is not complete, but it does serve to illustrate which functions should be locally administered and which should be centrally administered.

Local District	Central City
Garbage collection	Waste disposal[a]
Street cleaning	
Bulk pickup	
Delivery of social services	Delivery of welfare funds[b]

Local District	Central City
Housing management and maintenance	Housing construction[c]
	Housing financing[c]
Code enforcement	Relocation
	Housing standards
	Building construction codes
Local parking	Traffic
	Taxi regulation
Street maintenance, lighting	Main highways
Community hospitals	Teaching hospital complexes
Health services	
Outpatient clinics	Health research
	Health standards
	Epidemic control
Police precincts[d]	Police
Local nonviolent law enforcement	
Libraries, local	Libraries, central
	Firefighting
Local sewer maintenance[e]	Sewage treatment[a]
	Landmarks preservation
Local business	Commerce and industry
Local markets	Consumer protection
Local parks	Major parks
	Public utilities[a]
Air pollution code enforcement	Air pollution control standards
Cultural affairs, local	Cultural affairs
Personnel administration for local agencies	Civil service, collective bargaining
Local budget	City-wide budget
	Central managerial services

Local District	Central City
	Human rights
Planning implementation	Strategic City-wide
	planning
Local planning	Zoning[f]

[a]Waste disposal, sewage treatment, and power supply regulation could be considered regional functions. (See Chapter 7 for information on regional government.)

[b]Delivery of welfare funds is listed as a central function. Since the problems of poverty go beyond the borders of the City, and indeed are imposed upon the City by outside forces, delivery of welfare funds should preferably be a Federal function; the financial burden should not be the City's.

[c]Housing construction and financing might be a regional function.

[d]It is not intended to imply that the police precincts would devolve to local control, but that they would be correlated with the local districts and that their commanders would establish close liaison with the districts in which they function.

[e]If feasible.

[f]The Committee for Economic Development has suggested that zoning could be a shared function, with the larger unit empowered to specify broad areas of industrial, commercial and residential activity, which the local communities could zone into smaller areas.

REGIONAL FUNCTIONS

Ultimately, a variety of functions should be administered on a regional level, as indeed many of them already are (see also Chapter 7, "The Region").

Services Now Administered Regionally (wholly or partially)	Services That May Eventually Go to the Regional Level (some entirely, some as shared functions)
Mass transit	Regional economic development
Airline terminals	Water supply
Regional highways	Water pollution control
Interstate parks	Air pollution control

Services now Administered Regionally (wholly or partially)	Services that may Eventually go to the Regional Level (some entirely, some as shared functions)
Port and waterfront River crossings	Public utility regulation Waste disposal Regional land use planning Regional economic development Housing construction and financing

THE LOCAL DISTRICTS

When the structure and content of localized government are re-formulated, efficiency of service delivery must be blended with maximum participation of the local citizenry and maximum responsiveness of the governmental instruments. Therefore, the determination of district size is an unusually sensitive problem. There are no solid criteria for determining optimum district size in terms of either spatial configuration or population.

One study, sponsored by the Association of the Bar of the City of New York, carries the conclusion that each local government should serve a population of not less than 125,000 nor more than 300,000. This offers a range into which several of the existing planning and service districts could comfortably fit. There are 62 community planning districts, varying between 125,000 and 300,000 in population. There are 31 school districts, each of which averages 270,000 in population. Other service districts also fall within these population parameters.

While the community planning districts delineated by the City Planning Commission appear to be working relatively well, it is the conclusion of this Task Force that 62 local districts (based on the community planning district lines) would be too many. Approximately half that number, between 30 and 35 districts, could be set up under objective criteria and would provide local districts in the 200,000-300,000 range—large enough and strong enough to function, in effect, as middle-sized cities. There is general agreement that municipalities having populations within the 200,000-300,000 ambit are viable, governable, and of a size that promotes visibility of governmental operations, governmental responsiveness to citizens' needs, and easy public access to the instruments of government. Communities

of this size are large enough to inherit the advantages of proximity
and diversity that medium-sized cities tend to possess. They are
also sufficiently large to attain the advantages of economies of scale,
to plan within their borders, and to deliver the mix of services assigned to them. And yet, in the case of New York City, the communities—i.e., local districts—would be sufficiently small to permit the
City to remain a single entity powerful enough to make policy and
plan for the entire conurbation.

School district lines should, as soon as practicable, be correlated
with the proposed local district lines. This would be particularly
useful in the effort to involve local district government in the educational process and to coordinate local education with other local
governmental functions, such as child health services.*

The Existing Boroughs as a Possible
Basis for Local Districts

The suggestion has been made that the City should be subdivided
in such a way that the individual boroughs become the new local districts. A strong case can be made for such reorganization, and we
have examined the concept with great care. Our findings can be
summarized as follows:

—With the exception of Staten Island, the borough as the City's
basic subdivision would not achieve the objectives inherent in the
established principles and goals of localization.

—If each borough were granted full municipal service-delivery
prerogatives, the problems inherent in the delivery of services by
the City would remain, for there is little difference in the difficulties
besetting a municipal unit of 8 million people (the City) and a municipal
unit of 2 million people (a major borough).

—The citizen who is yearning for government that is less remote
and more accessible and responsive, for increased community participation in government, would not have his desires met in local districts as large as the present boroughs.

—With the borough as local district, there would be less effective
control over substantive functions for which even the entire City is
not sufficiently large—environmental protection, transportation,
scatter-site housing, etc. The minority groups might suffer from
increased restriction in mobility.

---

*It should be noted, however, that this proposal for local district
and school district correlation is not universally accepted. Some
school board members have expressed the view that present school
districts are too large.

FIGURE 8

Population of New York City (in thousands)

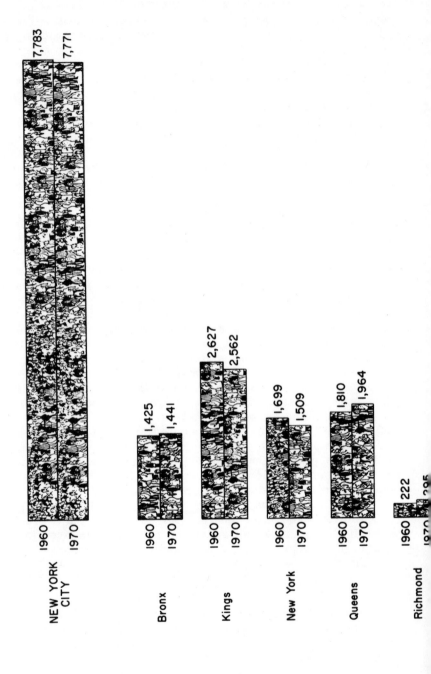

	1960	1970
NEW YORK CITY	7,783	7,771
Bronx	1,425	1,441
Kings	2,627	2,562
New York	1,699	1,509
Queens	1,810	1,964
Richmond	222	

In view of the above negative factors, we cannot accept the recommendation that the proposed local districts be based on the existing
five boroughs. As previously indicated, the need is for smaller units.
Even districts of 250,000 people should be further subdivided, for
local elections, for the purpose of achieving citizen participation,
and for a gain in local diversity.

Criteria for Delineation of Local Districts

The district lines should be plausible; they should be neither
arbitrary nor gerrymandered. The criteria that should guide the delineation of district lines should take into account the following factors:
    —existing traditional neighborhoods and patterns of neighbor-
hood organization;
    —geographical, geological, and topographic factors, such as
waterways, expressways, land contours;
    —suitability for planning of community life;
    —economic viability—that is, the presence of commercial or
industrial centers;
    —demographic factors, including population mix, ethnic com-
position, density;
    —existing community planning districts;
    —service-delivery lines, which, consistent with efficiency, should
be coterminous with local district lines;
    —transportation facilities and terminals.
    The Task Force has not attempted to draw district lines. That
is a process that will have to be undertaken at some later time.
    In the meantime, though, it is clear that the process of delineating
local districts is not impossibly complex; that a nonpolitical districting
body is fully capable of drawing the necessary lines; and that in drawing the lines, appropriate weight should be given to all of the factors
that went into the creation of the existing 62 community planning districts.

Possible Variations in Sizes of Local Districts

The Task Force has also considered the desirability of creating
local districts of varying sizes. It has been suggested that such
variations may be necessary in order to create districts that reflect
genuine existing community bases.
    The creation of districts with valid community bases is, of
course, a primary objective. If, however, the creation of such districts would require substantial deviation from a standard population

size, each such district could not be a councilmanic district for purposes of representation on the City Council without violation of the
one man-one vote rule.

Although it would be desirable for the local service districts to
be the same as the councilmanic districts, we do not believe that this
is a sufficiently important objective to justify disregarding existing
communities in the process of constructing the service districts.
At the same time, we do not know exactly what variations in population
may be necessary in order to use the existing communities as a basis
for establishing the service districts.

The solution to this dilemma will not come until an effort is
made to draw the district lines. If it develops that equal districts
cannot be drawn without doing violence to basic communities, we
would recommend creating local service districts of disparate sizes—
although preferably within the basic 200,000-300,000 population limits—
and creating separate and different councilmanic districts.

THE LOCAL COUNCIL

Under our formulation, there would be a locally elected council
in each local district.

Local Council Election

Council members would be elected from subdivisions of the
local district, each of the subdivisions having between 20,000 and
30,000 residents. Units of this size would assure fair representation
of the diverse ethnic and socioeconomic groups within the district.
The elected local council would thus consist of nine to twelve members.
We recommend a relatively small council rather than a large one, because a large council would be more costly without assuring better
results than a small one.

Elections would be held during the regular November election
period, with all members being elected for two-year terms. The
council members, who would serve on a part-time basis, would constitute the principal instrument of local citizen participation and control. They should be paid a nominal annual fee, perhaps in the
$5,000 to $7,500 range.

The Powers of the Local Council

The council would be empowered to determine the mix of services
for its district; the allocation of available financial resources; the
activities of inspection and code enforcement within the district; site

selection and planning implementation within the framework set by the central planning authorities; management and maintenance of public housing; overview of community corporations and other local quasi-governmental bodies; control of the district's governmental departments; appointment of committees and of such advisory bodies as it deemed necessary. In addition, the council would establish rules and regulations for service delivery. It would employ the local district executive, if the decision should be to have an appointed administrator. He, in turn, whether elected or appointed, would report regularly to the council and carry out its legislative mandates.

Each local council would prepare its own budget estimate and this would be collated and aligned with the budgets of other districts and the central City government. Each council would determine its own priorities within the revenues available to it (the budget process is described more fully in Chapter 5).

Competent staff assistance should be made available to the local council for all of the above-mentioned purposes.

Planning would be a shared central-local function. A local department of planning would be charged with responsibility and provided with resources to perform the essential planning functions for the district. Each such local department of planning would be independent of the central City's planning agency, taking its authority solely from the local council. Final decision-making on local planning matters would be a function of the local council (see Chapter 5).

The local government should be accorded purchasing flexibility. For example, it should be able to contract with the central government for the purchase of supplies and equipment; to combine with other districts to purchase elsewhere, if the needed products could be obtained at lower cost; or to purchase on its own. But its bills would be subject to audit by the City comptroller; if the prices paid by the district were higher than the prices at which the product could be obtained from the city, the district government officials would be subject to a penalty surcharge.

The Community Board

The community (planning) boards would remain. Each board would be, as it is at present, an advisory body, empowered to examine any matter affecting the interests of the local district. Its area of interest would coincide with the limits of the district. Its members could be appointed by the county executive (as they now are by the borough president), in which case they would perform a liaison function between the local district and the county executive in his central city relationship. Or the board members could be appointed either by the chairman of the local council (and consequently report to the council) or jointly by the county executive and the chairman of the local council. Each community board should act either upon the request of the appointing officer or upon its own initiative.

Politics and the Local District

The likelihood is that the traditional political parties would play a strong role in the local elections. This must be counted as a major asset of the local government system. The "out" party would have an interest in monitoring the work done by the party in power, and each party would have to compete for voter interest and approval. Furthermore, the parties would tend to develop candidates for office, which would constitute a vital element in the political health of the new local districts. The political parties would also have an interest in high voter registration, which means citizen participation. Yet, because the electoral subdivisions would be small, independent candidates would be able to obtain visibility even without political party endorsement.

Flexibility and Time

Much flexibility should be permitted the district council in organizing the local governments. Within the prescribed legislative limits, the local residents should be free to have the kind of municipal government they prefer, as do the people of any middle-sized U.S. city under state laws. But under no circumstances should the local council, as a collective body, attempt to take over day-to-day administration; the history of U.S. cities is replete with the failure of this kind of government.

The local district should also be allowed substantial time to organize a local government. Some areas of the City would be able to organize into viable governmental structures quickly; others would require substantial periods of transition time. Until a local district is sufficiently well organized to take on service delivery, the central government should continue to provide services for that district.

THE LOCAL DISTRICT ADMINISTRATION

The District Executive

Each local district would be headed by a chief executive, formally designated as either district executive or district director. He would either be elected by the general electorate or appointed by the local council, the choice of method being at the option of the district.

FIGURE 9

Proposed Organization of Local District Government

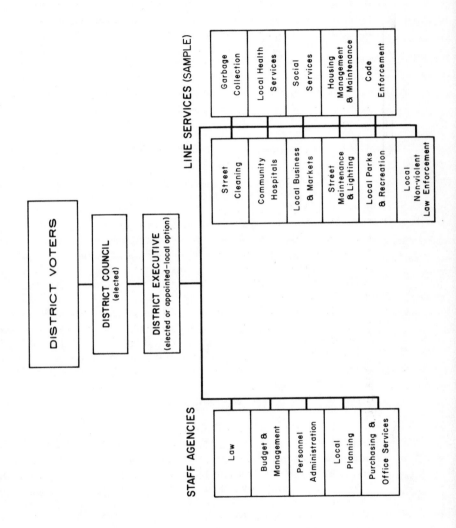

The duties and responsibilities of the district executive (irrespec-tive of the method by which he is selected) would be spelled out by the local council, to which he would report regularly and to which he would be held accountable. To operate effectively, the executive should have sufficient power to carry out the council's mandates and to manage the administration of local affairs. He should also have the managerial and staff tools needed to carry out his functions. Furthermore, he should be free from interference by the local council in his day-to-day operations.

The services to be administered locally have been described. The mix of services in each district would be determined by the local council on the basis of the district's needs.

The District's Administrative Structure

Under the supervision of the district executive, there would be administrative officers selected and employed by the local district to take charge of the various functions performed by the district. There would thus be district superintendents of street cleaning and garbage collection, of local non-violent law enforcement, of purchasing, of local parks and libraries and recreational facilities, of housing man-agement and maintenance and local code enforcement, of social and health services, and such others as are authorized. These would all be civil service employees.

The district executive would be responsible for the effective delivery of these services. And he would be in charge of such ad-ditional functions as may be assigned from time to time to the dis-tricts by the City Policy Board (the role of which is outlined in Chap-ter 4).

District Executive-City Councilman

At public hearings held by the Task Force, several witnesses suggested that the local district executive should be the city council-man elected from the district. The Task Force considered this pro-posal, with full understanding of the force of the recommendation. The city councilman would be working simultaneously for the local district as administrator and for the entire city as a legislator. The Task Force questions whether these dual functions could be coordi-nated effectively. It is also apprehensive that city policy—particularly budgetary matters—would suffer from such an arrangement, since the district executive-city councilman would inevitably be locally oriented (it being the local district constituency that elects him to office).

Another question arises: would the local executive have sufficient time to perform both jobs? In response to this point, the suggestion has been made that the executive-councilman should have under him a trained administrator to carry out day-to-day functions. But this, too, suffers the disability of duplicated effort.

The Task Force concludes that the office of district executive and the office of city councilman should not be combined.

Citizen-Government Communication

One of the important reasons for decentralization is the need for making government more accessible to the people. Accessibility requires proximity, which means that each local district would have a central communication office, attached directly to that of the district executive. This office would be a "little city hall" in the true sense, for it would receive and process complaints, suggestions, comments, and calls for service. The ideal arrangement would be for every citizen to find this office, or subdivisions of it, within walking distance of his home.

In addition, for all his local needs, the local citizen should have a single telephone number to call. That this is possible is indicated by the fact that the City has been able to establish various single numbers to serve everyone in the entire New York City area requiring a particular service.

THE NEIGHBORHOOD
SERVICE REPRESENTATIVE

Each local district would have a corps of local, part-time law enforcement officials, who would be known as neighborhood service representatives. Although not part of the official police force these officials would undertake duties directed at dealing with nonviolent, antisocial activities in the district, particularly violations of the parking, sanitation, and air pollution laws.

The neighborhood service representatives would perform a variety of local tasks that are now poorly done or not done at all. They would be residents of their areas, people familiar with the conditions on the streets. They would report illegal emissions from chimneys and smokestacks, and, where appropriate, they would be authorized to issue summonses. They would also be empowered to ticket illegally parked or double-parked cars; give warnings or summonses to landlords who do not abide by the laws requiring sidewalks to be kept clean and in good repair, and garbage to be kept in containers; report to the police any criminal activities they may witness;

report potholes in the streets or back-up of sewers; give summonses to citizens whose dogs befoul sidewalks; direct citizens to proper headquarters for complaints or assistance; locate help for the aged and handicapped; assist the regular City-wide and local inspectors in the performance of their duties; keep the local council informed of the general physical condition of their areas. The neighborhood service representatives would constitute, in effect, a continuous district government "presence" in the areas to which they are assigned.

The position would not require great expertise. It should be open to residents of the local district, and it might be a useful post particularly for recently returned veterans and qualified people on the welfare rolls who are subject to the new "workfare" laws.

We regard the concept of the neighborhood service representative as a critical part of our proposal for re-structuring the city government. This one aspect would go a long way toward giving to local governmental entities a vitality in their communities that is largely missing from the City scene of today.

4

THE CENTRAL GOVERNMENT

The central governmental level of New York City would consist of two executives, the mayor and the comptroller; the City Policy Board; and the City Council. The central City government would retain responsibility for all decisions of City-wide or inter-district significance.

THE MAYORALTY IN A TWO-TIER SYSTEM

New York City has a "strong mayor" tradition. Our proposal does not involve scrapping that tradition. But we believe New York's tradition should be reviewed in light of the way in which other world cities deal with the problem of executive power.

How Executive Power Works Elsewhere

If one examines the executive functions of major world cities, one finds that cities operate in many ways.

—London has no single chief executive. There is the Greater London Council, which supervises matters that are regional; and 32 boroughs, that manage a great variety of local services.

—Certain German cities have a council and an Oberstaatsdirektor, somewhat like the American city manager. Again, there is a second level of government for local services.

—Tokyo has a strong metropolitan governor, managing those services which affect the people of the entire region; there are also 23 local service delivery districts which have jurisdiction over various local services.

—Paris has no mayor; there are prefects, appointed by the national government. And there are the <u>arrondissements</u>, where people go for a variety of personal services.

—Toronto has a metropolitan government headed by a chairman elected by a metropolitan area council. Distribution of responsibilities between metropolitan tier and local tiers is clearly spelled out.

—Shanghai has a central municipal government, and ten sub-divisions dealing with local matters.

It is customary in many cities for the more important government tier to be the "lower" one, the one that deals most immediately with the intimate needs of the residents.

Thus, one finds in the world's major cities strong executives and weak ones. Whatever the form, the history, tradition, national government, and population of the cities determine the executive structure. Not only mayors or their equivalents are executives. City councils sometimes take on executive functions; there are executives appointed by local councils; elected committees with executive functions; municipal executives appointed by central governments.

In New York City, as indeed elsewhere in the United States, the trend during the twentieth century has been toward a concentration of executive power. The rationale for this has been that authority and responsibility should be intertwined. It was said, during the conferences on the 1961 New York City Charter, "Since the mayor gets the blame anyway, he ought to have the authority." This point of view was accepted: Executive power, where it did not already reside in the office of the mayor, was transferred there. The 1961 Charter gave to the mayor more power than he had ever had before and provided him with the tools to exercise that power.

A Governmental System Designed for New York City

We have examined models of various approaches to municipal executive management. Much is to be learned from them. But none of these models can be transferred to New York City. We must begin with this City's own, unique characteristics—its mix, its history, its geography, and its intergovernmental relations.

The Task Force had developed a plan that differs from other proposed structures in a fundamental way: it proposes a system of viable local governments while establishing a framework in which the mayor supervises the City's central services and heads its major governing unit. It may well be that this formulation would give the City of New York a mayor of stronger potential than that which the present Charter permits. At the same time, the plan satisfies the citizen demand for government that is less remote and more responsive and accessible.

It is not the intention of the authors of this report to fragment the City of New York or its central government. Under the Task Force's proposed two-tier arrangement, there would continue to be a modified strong-mayor system, in that the City's size, interrelationships, complexity, population mix, problems, and needs require the leadership of a strong central executive. The two approaches—strong central leadership and local district government—are, in the Task Force's opinion, both compatible and feasible.

If it is to exercise the planning, policy, and program wisdom the City demands, the mayoralty must retain its formal executive power as well as the more subtle power the system confers upon that office. A mayor freed from the cares and details of day-to-day routine administration is able to exercise these policy and decision-making roles more effectively. This would become even clearer if day-to-day administration were carried out at levels that would absolve the mayor from intrusion and intervention in every little service-delivery dispute. This point of view was expressed in a report prepared for Mayor John V. Lindsay in 1966. The report said that:

> Today, the Mayor maintains not only ultimate authority and responsibility for the formulation and execution of planning, housing, and development programs; by virtue of the current administrative disorder, he is, in fact, their day-to-day administrator. This is an unfair, unwise and unnecessary burden. In New York City, mayoral injunctions to cooperate, mayoral executive orders to coordinate have only limited impact for a limited time.
>   The pressing need for decentralization is equally important. New York City is too big to be governed effectively from offices in the vicinity of City Hall. City government must be brought closer to the people, particularly to those who live in slums and blighted areas.
>   Many New Yorkers, particularly those in the ghettos, feel alienated from their government. An overly centralized government in a City as large as New York cannot help but be unresponsive and difficult to reach. . . .[5]

Role of the Mayor

The mayor would remain the chief executive officer of the central City government, retaining all the powers he now holds over the line agencies of the central government tier. A budget office would be under his jurisdication to deal with the budgets of the central agencies.

He would retain the authority to create or abolish bureaus, divisions, and positions within his executive office as he deems necessary to fulfill his duties. The mayor would also retain his considerable powers of appointment, being able to appoint—without confirmation from any other body—deputies to assist him, as well as heads of all departments under his jurisdiction. Through these top appointments, the mayor would continue to exercise direction over the priorities and activities of the central line agencies. With the assistance of the Mayor's Committee on the Judiciary, the mayor would also continue to make judicial appointments.

The mayor would preside over the City Policy Board, exercising a weighted vote on that board because his constituency is City-wide and because he is the elected chief executive officer of the entire City. As chairman of the Policy Board, he would continue to maintain a vital role in preparing the City's total capital and expense budgets. In addition, as chairman of the Policy Board, the mayor would participate in the resolution of conflicts between local and central agencies, in the reassignment of functions and services when experience shows these changes to be necessary, and in all other actions of the board. In all of these actions, the mayor would exercise his weighted vote indicating that he represents the entire City.

The staff agencies responsible to the City Policy Board would report administratively to the mayor. The mayor would appoint the chief officers of these agencies with the approval of the Policy Board. Also, since the mayor would be both chairman of the Policy Board and chief executive officer of the City, the services of the staff agencies would be available to him in matters affecting the central City departments (the mayor's role in the shared functions of budget planning and administration are spelled out in Chapter 5).

The mayor would exercise substantial influence over both central and local service-agency operations, conditions, and budgets through his role as City negotiator in collective bargaining with municipal unions. Collective bargaining would continue as a central function, being conducted by the Office of Labor Relations with the assistance of the Office of Collective Bargaining.

The mayor would be spokesman for the entire City in relations with the State and Federal governments, in relations with public authorities and with other municipalities in dealing with the City's economy, and in all other matters affecting the City as a whole. Since it is almost inevitable that an increasingly large proportion of New York City's revenues will be obtained from Federal and State sources, the mayor's role as City spokesman and negotiator for these grants will become increasingly important—and time-consuming. And as central spokesman for the City, the Mayor would continue to have wide access to the media for presenting his views and advocating his policies.

FIGURE 10

New York City's Former Governmental Structure (and Executive Agencies) Prior to 1966

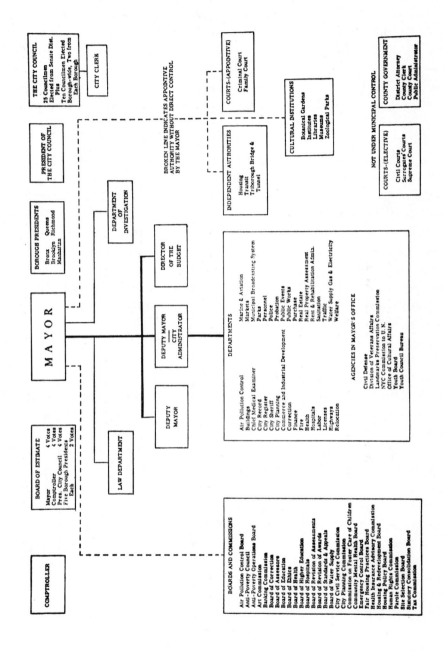

COMPTROLLER

BOARD OF ESTIMATE
Mayor   4 Votes
Comptroller   4 Votes
Pres. City Council   4 Votes
Five Borough Presidents
Each   2 Votes

DEPUTY MAYOR

LAW DEPARTMENT

MAYOR

BOROUGH PRESIDENTS
Bronx   Queens
Brooklyn   Richmond
Manhattan

DEPARTMENT OF INVESTIGATION

DEPUTY MAYOR CITY ADMINISTRATOR

DIRECTOR OF THE BUDGET

PRESIDENT OF THE CITY COUNCIL

THE CITY COUNCIL
25 Councilmen
Elected from Senate Dist.
Plus
Ten Councilmen Elected
Borough-wide, Two from
Each Borough

CITY CLERK

BROKEN LINE INDICATES APPOINTIVE
AUTHORITY WITHOUT DIRECT CONTROL
BY THE MAYOR

COURTS—(APPOINTIVE)
Criminal Court
Family Court

DEPARTMENTS
Air Pollution Control
Buildings
Chief Medical Examiner
City Record
City Register
City Sheriff
City Planning
Commerce and Industrial Development
Correction
Finance
Fire
Health
Hospitals
Labor
Licenses
Highways
Relocation
Marine & Aviation
Markets
Municipal Broadcasting System
Parks
Personnel
Police
Probation
Public Events
Public Works
Purchase
Real Estate
Real Property Assessment
Rent & Rehabilitation Admin.
Sanitation
Traffic
Water Supply Gas & Electricity
Welfare

AGENCIES IN MAYOR'S OFFICE
Civil Defense
Division of Veterans Affairs
Landmarks Preservation Commission
NYC Commission to U. N.
Office of Cultural Affairs
Youth Board
Youth Council Bureau

INDEPENDENT AUTHORITIES
Housing
Transit
Triborough Bridge &
Tunnel

CULTURAL INSTITUTIONS
Botanical Gardens
Institutes
Libraries
Museums
Zoological Parks

BOARDS AND COMMISSIONS
Air Pollution Control Board
Anti-Poverty Council
Anti-Poverty Operations Board
Art Commission
Banking Commission
Board of Correction
Board of Assessors
Board of Education
Board of Ethics
Board of Health
Board of Higher Education
Board of Hospitals
Board of Revision of Assessments
Board of Revision of Awards
Board of Standards & Appeals
Board of Water Supply
City Civil Service Commission
City Planning Commission
Commission on Foster Care of Children
Community Mental Health Board
Emergency Control Board
Fair Housing Practices Board
Health Insurance Advisory Commission
Housing & Redevelopment Board
Housing Policy Board
Human Rights Commission
Parole Commission
Site Selection Board
Statutory Consolidation Board
Tax Commission

NOT UNDER MUNICIPAL CONTROL

COUNTY GOVERNMENT
District Attorney
County Clerk
County Court
Public Administrator

COURTS—(ELECTIVE)
Civil Courts
Surrogates' Courts
Supreme Court

47

FIGURE 11

New York City's Present Governmental Structure

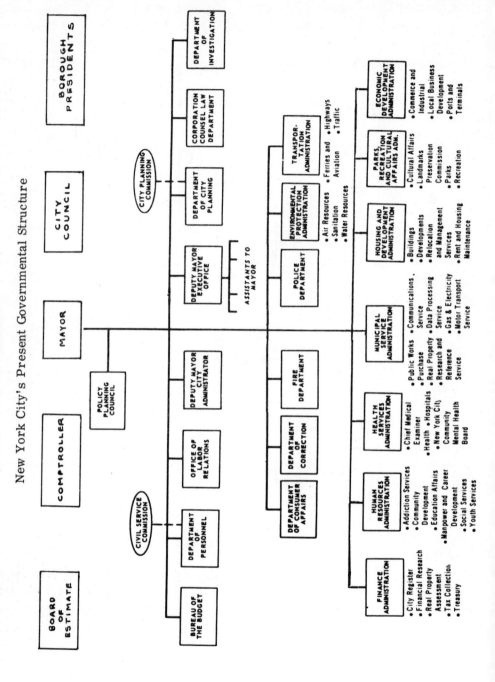

FIGURE 12

The Task Force's Proposal for a Two-Level
Governmental Structure for New York City

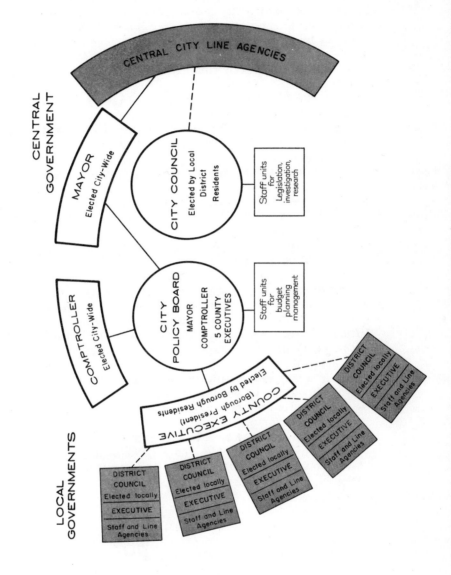

The devolution of responsibility for many of the functions of day-to-day service delivery to community districts would free the mayor to devote greater attention to pressing issues of City-wide concern. Transfer of many of the mayor's routine duties and worries would enable him to concentrate on improving the economic revenue base of the City by attracting and holding business activity, to develop legislative packages for State or Federal legislation affecting the City, and to engage in other activities that affect the long-range vitality of the entire City.

At a public hearing held by this Task Force, Borough President Sebastian Leone of Brooklyn, in the course of advocating a decentralized government structure for New York City, enunciated an opinion that meshes with that of the Task Force concerning the mayor's role. Mr. Leone stated:

"As we consider these proposals for progressively localizing our government, there is one question which is certain to be raised and it is this: After years of fighting for a chief executive at the head of a highly centralized government, are we now going to weaken the effectiveness of the mayor, and undermine the efficiency of the City-wide municipal establishment by pointing responsibility in the direction of the local neighborhoods?

"I would like to answer that question in this way. By freeing the mayor from the nagging drudgery of service and maintenance functions—by freeing him from neighborhood decision-making and local disputes, we strengthen the institution of the mayoralty itself. By lifting from the central government the burden of operations that cannot be efficiently administered on a City-wide basis, we enable it to function in its proper sphere.

"In a city of 8 million people, the greatest city on earth, the mayor should not be concerned with yesterday's garbage. He should be dealing with tomorrow's destiny.

"The mayor of New York should be free to concentrate on high-level planning and the broad aspects of municipal administration. He should be a leader, a guide, and a spokesman for a proud city. His voice should be heard with authority in capitals of the State and the nation."

THE COMPTROLLER

The comptroller would continue to be a City-wide elected independent officer empowered to audit, to probe financial transactions, and to report upon the financial condition of the central City—as well as of the proposed new local districts.

The comptroller should retain, with one exception, all the powers he now holds and be vested with an additional surcharge power described below. As the Charter now mandates, he should advise the mayor, the City Council, and the City Policy Board on the financial condition of the City and to make recommendations concerning fiscal policy and financial transactions. In addition, he should invest City funds, settle claims, keep the City's accounts, manage the City's trust funds and sinking funds, float City bonds, and pay the City's bills.

Local districts should handle their own financial affairs insofar as possible. Their authority should include the payment of district bills—for without these powers, the whole concept of district government is hollow. However, the districts should be able to contract with the City comptroller for payroll and other services, at least during the initial years while the new governments are being set up. Furthermore, the comptroller should post-audit the district government expenditures (as well as those of the central City government) and invest their funds.

We also recommend that he be vested with the additional power to surcharge district officials whom he finds to have misspent public funds. The burden would be on the public official to justify his conduct. Thus, if a local district purchased materials from a particular source at a price higher than that at which they could have been bought from the central purchasing agency, and if the district cannot justify its action, the comptroller would have the power to penalize the local officials who participated in the decision, surcharging them for the difference between the City's available price and the price actually paid. Any such surcharges, though, would be subject to judicial review.

We also recommend that consideration be given to depriving the comptroller of the pre-audit function. This function has been criticized over the years as slowing the payment of bills and as serving no useful purpose that is not as well served by the comptroller's post-audit function.

One suggestion made to the Task Force is that the comptroller remain an elected official, but without a seat on the Board of Estimate (or its successor agency). He would be the City's chief auditor, as at present, but he would be independent, performing his investigations without being involved in matters upon which, as a board member, he would have to vote from time to time. The Task Force has considered this suggestion, but recognizes a strong case for maintaining the present arrangement. The checks-and-balances approach, in which the comptroller plays a useful role, suggests that there ought to be, in addition to the mayor, another official, elected City-wide, on the board. Moreover, the special expertise that the comptroller brings to the board is a desirable asset in the decision-making process. We therefore recommend that the comptroller remain a member of the board, with a weighted vote reflecting his City-wide constituency.

Nevertheless, if the ultimate decision of a charter commission is to separate the comptroller from the board, making him an independent elected official (perhaps reporting to both the City Policy Board and to the City Council), this would not impair the general plan of the two-level governmental structure as proposed by the Task Force.

THE CITY POLICY BOARD

In creating a plan for re-structuring the City's governmental system, the Task Force has allowed for the use of existing governmental instruments wherever possible, rather than creating wholly new ones. In line with this principle, we recommend that the Board of Estimate be transformed into a new institution of government called the City Policy Board.

Membership of the City Policy Board would consist of five county executives, elected borough-wide from the five existing boroughs (which are coextensive with five existing counties); the mayor, elected City-wide; and the comptroller, elected City-wide. In light of the difference between borough-wide and City-wide constituencies, voting power on the Policy Board should be weighted, with the balance resting on the side of the City-wide officials.

General Comment

At its public hearings, the Task Force found, among certain segments of the New York public, distrust of the Board of Estimate and a reluctance to accept it or any successor group as the major governing body of municipal government. The Task Force cannot recognize such distrust as a valid objection. Upon close questioning of those who harbor this view, it becomes clear that critics of the board are frequently unable to delineate its functions and duties, have no realistic concept of its role as a deliberative body open to all residents of the City, nor of the many essential activities it performs and judgments it makes that have to be performed and made. It is the view of the Task Force that, far from being a body unworthy of major responsibility, the Board of Estimate is in fact a unique instrument of governmental viability.

In the plan which the Task Force proposes, a "balance-wheel" agency between central and local governmental relationships is required; otherwise, the local governments would become either increasingly impotent, eventually being swallowed up by the central government; or, through City councilmen elected locally, so powerful as to annihilate the viability of the central government. A strong agency between central and local governments is needed to perform those functions that the board now performs, in addition to substantial new functions. If such an agency did not exist, it would have to be invented. We prefer that the existing instrument, the Board of Estimate, be remolded into the City Policy Board, with new and unprecedented responsibilities and obligations.

Roles of the City Policy Board

As envisioned by the Task Force, the City Policy Board would undertake a variety of roles. The principal roles are:

—The board would mediate conflicts in relationships between the central and local governments, and among the district governments.

—The board would have power to transfer a function either from the districts to the central government or from the central government to the districts; it would also have the power to recommend that the function go instead to a regional or state level, if a determination were made that the function could be better performed at another level. Indeed, this is one of the most important aspects of the proposed structure. It provides essential flexibility and constitutes a needed safety factor. For should it develop that jurisdiction over certain functions had been unwisely allocated either to the local or central level initially, the allocation could be reviewed and changed by the Policy Board.

—The individual county executives would have overview responsibilities with respect to the districts in their respective boroughs. Furthermore, upon their initiative, the Policy Board would have the power to apply corrective measures in cases of malfeasance, misfeasance, or gross inefficiency in district governance; this power would include that of supersession where appropriate.

—The Policy Board's general powers of oversight and supersession would include the power to create an entity such as the Emergency Control Board, which, in turn, would be empowered, in emergencies, to direct local districts to make certain manpower and equipment available to other districts. Thus, for example, if there were a plane crash in a given district and manpower and equipment were quickly needed far in excess of those available within the district, the Emergency Control Board could direct other districts to make facilities and employees temporarily available to help deal with the crisis.

—The City Policy Board would share budget-preparation powers with the mayor, would supervise the development of budgetary allocation formulas for the local district governments, and would resolve conflicts of budgetary allocation between the central and district government tiers (see Chapter 5).

—The board would share with the City Council the obligation to fix the annual real estate tax rate.

—The board would have a vital rate in the mixed central-local planning decision process.

—Although control of local streets would pass to the local district governments, the Board of Estimate's current exclusive power to grant franchises should be retained by the successor City Policy Board in instances where these franchises concern inter-district facilities, on the surface and underground, including railroads, pipes and other conduits, and cables used for the transmission of power.

—The City Policy Board would assume other responsibilities held by the Board of Estimate, including the granting of leases for City property, assignment of City property for public use, approval of contracts, and related matters now assigned to the Board of Estimate under the terms of the Charter. However, where such matters may properly be devolved to the local districts in keeping with the principles of district responsibility, provisions should be made for transferral to the local governments.

There have been suggestions that the Policy Board be given certain administrative powers, now held by mayoral agencies. The Task Force rejects these suggestions. They would merely create an additional level of government without any perceptible gain that would not accrue by giving the authority and responsibility directly to the local governments or by allowing these powers to remain with the mayoralty.

Moreover, the roles assigned to the City Policy Board make it a body unique in municipal governance, with a depth and variety of functions that would fully occupy its members. Their involvement in the planning, budgetary, management, and oversight processes would be far greater than that of current Board of Estimate members. These Policy Board roles should not be diluted by the inclusion of administrative duties.

The Task Force recommends granting to the City Policy Board the tools that would enable it to carry out its tasks effectively. Since the Policy Board would have broad responsibilities in the fields of planning, budget, and in management, we recommend that a planning review office, a management staff, and budget staff be assigned to the board. Such staffing will be essential if the board is properly to perform its budgetary and administrative roles that are now performed wholly by the mayor, as well as its role in the planning area, where the Board of Estimate has always had a function but never a staff.

In the proposed budgetary process, for example, the mayor's role over the central service agencies would continue unchanged, as would his role in estimating revenues and proposing revenue sources.

But the Policy Board would become the arbiter of the amounts to be allocated to the districts, so the Policy Board would need a staff budget arm.

Similarly, just as the mayor requires management services to properly administer the central service agencies, so the Policy Board members—specificially, the county executives—would also need similar management services in order to properly oversee the districts and to provide them with the administrative assistance they may request.

Although the central planning function is one over which the mayor would remain the executive chief, it is a function that would require Policy Board participation in order to approve central City plans and to resolve disagreements between central and local planning activities. To perform these functions, the Policy Board would need a small planning-review staff of its own.

If budgeting, administration, and planning were to remain solely mayoral functions, then the mayor, through his staff, would have the power to control the local districts. On the other hand, suggestions that these three functions be defined as Policy Board functions, with the mayor directing them as chairman of the Policy Board, have been viewed by some as an unwise weakening of mayoral authority.

The solution we propose is a division of staff functions, providing both the mayoralty and the Policy Board with the assistance that each requires to carry out its functions. The result would be clear mayoral authority over the central service level, clear mayoral prerogative in the formulation of the parts of the budget for which the mayor is responsible, and clear mayoral prerogative in initiating City-wide strategic planning. At the same time, adequate staffing provided to the Policy Board would enable it to perform its function as balance wheel, adjudicator, overseer of the local districts, and participant in the budgetary process. It is the checks-and-balances concept applied to municipal government.

City Policy Board Voting Alternatives

The Task Force has considered various weighted voting patterns. One suggestion would give the mayor four votes, the comptroller two votes, and each county executive one vote. This would provide a total of six votes for the City-wide officials and five votes for the officials elected by county-wide constituencies.

Another plan proposes the equalization of votes between the City-wide officials and those elected county-wide. One such formula would give the mayor and the comptroller five votes each, and the five county executives a total of five votes.

Still a third formula would give the mayor eight votes, the comptroller four votes, and to the county executives two votes each.

A fourth proposal holds that there should be a relationship between voting power on the City Policy Board and population.

The Task Force makes no recommendation at this time, other than to indicate that weighted voting is practicable and that a differential between the county and City-wide officials should be retained, in light of the differences between borough-wide and City-wide constituencies.

THE COUNTY EXECUTIVE

The Task Force proposes that each borough president be replaced by a county executive. He would be elected by voters within the borders of his present county.

In addition to serving as a member of the City Policy Board, the county executive would have overview responsibilities of the local districts within his county. Where a district is operating poorly, failing in the delivery of services, or demonstrating fiscal irresponsibility, the Policy Board would be empowered—upon request of the appropriate county executive and following proper objective findings—to direct that certain local functions or an entire local council be temporarily superseded.*

The staffs made available to the City Policy Board for planning, budgetary, and management purposes would also be available to each county executive in carrying out his overview responsibilities and his policy prerogatives.

The county executive would play a dual role under the new system: as policy-maker through his membership on the Policy Board, and as intermediary between the central City government and the local district governments within his borough. As participant in the budget-making process, he would act in a balance-wheel capacity among the various local and City-wide interests.

The county executive would also serve on regional bodies, such as the Metropolitan Regional Council, as does the Mayor. Since chief executive officers of the outlying counties already serve on these bodies, admission of the City's five county executives into membership

---

*In practice, this would not mean the assumption of operational power by the Policy Board. Rather, the board would probably designate a temporary overseer of the district or direct its management experts to put things in order locally.

would make for a more equitable arrangement; it would also facilitate cooperation between the five New York City counties and the suburban counties in working on mutually desirable projects. It is a reasonable assumption that the entry of the county executives into regional affairs alongside their counterparts from the other counties in the metropolitan region would tend to strengthen efforts toward devising and implementing regional approaches to regional problems.

During the Task Force hearings, the suggestion was frequently repeated that any new devolution of functions and services ought to be to the borough presidents; opposition to the idea was also heard. Generally, the residents of Queens and Richmond seemed inclined to give operating powers to the borough president, while residents from the other three boroughs strongly preferred smaller service-delivery units.

With the exception of Richmond, however, the boroughs are too populous to serve the basic units of local government. Governing Brooklyn, centrally, with its 2,600,000 residents, would not, in our judgment, constitute any improvement over governing New York City, with its 7,800,000 people, centrally.

Borough President Leone of Brooklyn apparently agrees with this view. At a public hearing of the Task Force, he recommended the creation of districts of approximately 150,000 people per district.

Moreover, while Queens residents and officials appeared to view the problem of service delivery and accountability in their own borough as attributable to the pro-Manhattan bias of the central government, Manhattanites actually have the same kinds of problems in securing adequate services. If there were a transfer of functions to the borough level in Queens, it seems clear to us that within a few years it would become evident that a 2-million population base is too large to effectively deliver local services in a New York City borough; the demand for local participation within portions of the borough would inevitably grow.

It may well be that it will take longer for Queens to set up and make operational the local districts we propose. But we believe that, like the other four boroughs, Queens would be better off with government more localized than it would be if service delivery were returned to the borough level.

THE CITY COUNCIL

Role of the City Council

Under the proposed re-structuring system, the City Council would retain all the powers it presently holds:

—The council would remain the City-wide legislative body.

—It would retain its investigative powers.

—It would approve the budget, no longer sharing this authority with the Board of Estimate (or its successor, the City Policy Board). The Policy Board's budget role would be exercised in the preparation process.

The fixing of annual tax rates would be a shared function, exercised by the Council and by the Policy Board. Since both are engaged in the budget process, both should share responsibility for tax rates.

The Task Force recommends reorganization of the council committee system in order to relate the committees to the work of the City-wide mayoral agencies and thus make of the council a more knowledgeable and more effective body than it is today. The plan envisions functional Council committees, with a committee for each major central City activity. The heads of City-wide agencies would report to their Council committees; the committees would remain alert to the activities of departments under their jurisdiction, and they could recommend changes in departmental policies to either the department heads or the mayor.

While policy of City-wide agencies would remain within the domain of the mayor, proposed budgets of the agencies would be reviewed by the relevant City Council committees before being submitted to the central budget officials.

The committee-agency arrangement would result in growing expertise within the Council in specific functional areas; require the agency head to keep himself informed because he would be reporting regularly to a knowledgeable legislative group; and provide the councilmen and councilwomen with greater power in dealing with the agencies on behalf of their constituents. There is further advantage in tying together, within a two-tier system, the various echelons of the two governmental levels in a government working with checks and balances.

Strengthening the City Council

The City Council should be strengthened effectively to perform its varied roles. This means stronger staffing than the council now possesses. The staff would assist in careful evaluation of the budget, advise the council on its legal relationships with other City agencies and with the State, assist in preparation of legislative bills and reports, make the investigative function more thorough and meaningful than it has been, and keep the council committees continually informed of all relevant matters affecting the whole City and the local districts.

The New York City Council is restricted by the State, which holds the fundamental power, in the legislation that it can enact. Nevertheless, given these new roles and these new instruments, the City Council could well become a strengthened, more effective legislative body for the City.

Councilmanic Elections

The councilmanic districts should be coextensive with local districts if this is legally permissible. If not, the councilmanic districts should conform as closely as possible to the local district lines. The final consideration is the one man-one vote ruling of the United States Supreme Court. At the time of this writing, it is not yet certain whether it will be possible to make City Council electoral districts coextensive with local service districts, as this Task Force recommends, since the proposed service district boundaries are based more on logical community areas than on close equality of population size.

It has been suggested to the Task Force that the City councilman also be designated the executive head of the district from which he is elected. However, if it is necessary to spread the councilmanic electoral districts over more than one local service district, a councilman could not also be a local district executive for any one district.

The Task Force recommends that the present arrangement of ten councilmen elected on a borough-wide basis be abandoned. In practice, at-large or borough-elected councilmen have no powers different from those of councilmen elected from the councilmanic districts. The original rationale for the system of borough-wide councilmen, which was to provide some minority-party representation on the council, disappears in the structure we propose.

The Council President

The role of the president of the City Council is largely ministerial. He presides over meetings of the Council, but, with the exception of his membership on the Board of Estimate, he has no other legal power. His position as "vice mayor" should be eliminated, nor should he hold membership on the proposed City Policy Board. The Task Force recommends that the City Council members elect their own presiding officer.

5

THE EXPENSE BUDGET

The executive budget is a formidable—perhaps the most formidable—instrument of governmental power. It can be used, and has been used, by mayors to provide political rewards and to administer political punishment. It can be used, and has been used, to thwart policies that have apparently been approved. And whether in its simple line-item form, arrayed as a performance budget, or in its more fashionable Program-Planning-Budgeting Systems (PPBS) format, the document is rarely visible in all of its particulars. It is possible to hide money in it in most ingenious ways. A clever budget examiner may do so in such a manner that not even the mayor, whoever he may be, will know exactly where certain funds are. Middle-level budget examiners are able to modify, or even kill, programs that represent high policy decision. A New York Times article described certain aspects of the budget process as follows:

" 'I've been here for almost two years, and I'm just learning where they hide the money,' Alan Claxton, an assistant budget director, commented recently. 'It's all coded. . . . ' The found money and lost jobs are all part of a budget process that is understood by only a handful of officials. . . . The scope of the proposed budget—$9.5 billion to be given 87 city agencies that employ 400,000 people—almost guarantees that detailed comprehension is beyond the grasp of almost everyone else, including high officials in the Budget Bureau. . . . "6

The Task Force on Jurisdiction and Structure proposes to make the New York City budget wholly visible. We feel that the City's budget,—which exceeds that of most nations of the world, demands visibility. The people should know what they are paying and to whom. More directly, the decision-makers should know. The fact that, under existing procedures, budgets have never seen major change is a fair indication that those who approve the executive budget have neither the tools nor the expertise to analyze it properly and act upon it intelligently. And if a budget is to be devised for the central City and for a substantial number of local districts as well, the need for visibility and clarity becomes even more imperative.

Without some financial responsibility exercised by the districts, local government cannot be viable, because power inevitably flows to resource-control capability. Therefore, four premises must be posited:

1. The central City government must retain budgetary powers over functions allocated to it.

2. The local district governments must have budgetary powers over their functions.

3. A satisfactory plan of resource allocation between the two levels must be developed.

4. A decision-making unit must be built into the plan to deal with conflicts and to resolve competing demands for limited resources.

A Proposal for Budget-Making

The Task Force proposes the following model.

The Instruments of Budget

The instruments to be used in the budget-making process as formulated by the Task Force would be as follows:

—The central Budget Office remains under the mayor, as at present, performing the budgetary functions of the central government.

—Local budget offices are attached to each district to undertake the local budgeting.

—A small Division of Budget Policy is created, to be the budgetary arm of the City Policy Board.

Budget Preparation

Two budgets are prepared separately. One for the central City government is prepared by the central Budget Office; the other, a combination of all the local district budgets, is prepared by the local budget offices.

The Central City Budget. This is prepared as it is at present—by way of budget requests assembled by each of the central agencies and submitted for review to the central Budget Office.

The Local District Budgets. The district budgets, being new, require a new approach. Prior to the preparation of the district budgets, a revenue-sharing formula, to be applied to each district, has to be devised. This formula would allot each district a fixed percentage of the total revenue to be allocated to the local government tier. Among factors to go into the formula would be such items as the following:

—mandatory payments for fixed salaries, pensions, and other employee benefits;

—essential equipment and materials;

—miles of streets to be cleaned and frequency of cleaning;

—population density;

—daytime and night-time populations;

—number of children, plus required children's services;

—number of aged, handicapped, and indigent, plus services required for them;

—maintenance of parks, and recreational and cultural activities;

—activities peculiar to the district, such as unusual quantities of public housing requiring management and maintenance;

—cost of local government;

—a basic special purpose fund for the district to use as it sees fit.

Under this formula, determination of the precise amount of revenue to be allocated to each district becomes a largely mechanical process, once the total to be made available to the districts is fixed. And each district would know how much money it would have available during the year for its operations. In case of special need, a district could request an increase in its percentage allocation—but, in that case, it would know that its additional funds must come from a reduction in the allocations of the other districts or of the central City government.

A Hypothetical Case. Let us examine a hypothetical case of budget preparation and fund allocation under the revenue-sharing formula. Let us assume that a total of 30 percent of the anticipated revenues would be allocated to the local districts, 70 percent to the central City government. Let us assume further, in this hypothetical case, that there are 30 district governments and that the anticipated revenues—to be divided among these 30 units and the central government—total $1,000. Of this sum, 70 percent, or $700, would be allocated to the activities of the central government. The remaining $300 would be shared, according to the formula, by the 30 district governments. But the needs of the districts would not be the same. The formula would mean that different percentages apply to the different districts, with each district's allocation being determined according to its needs. Assume that District A is allocated 2 percent;

it would then receive, for the fiscal year, the sum of $6 (that is, 2 percent of $300). If its allocation were 3 percent, it would receive $9.

Devising and Approving the Revenue-Sharing Formulas. Who would devise the formulas and who would approve them? The budgetary arm of the Policy Board would prepare the formulas, supplying the board with the information it would require. The ultimate decisions would then be made by the board, which represents both local and central interests. The mayor, with his weighted vote, sits on the board, so the central governmental interests would be protected. Clearly, there would be negotiation, as there is today. Traditionally, departments of the City government make their annual requests, assemble their support, and then struggle against the inevitable reductions which the Budget Bureau imposes in order to stay within the anticipated revenues. The same thing would happen in this proposed scheme, only now the districts would endeavor to raise their percentages on the basis of special needs or special programs.

Subsequently, the City Policy Board would propose the annual budget, which is the combination of the central budget and of the local budgets. From the board, the proposed budget would then go to the City Council.

The Budgetary Arm of the City Policy Board. The Division of Budget Policy, the proposed budgetary arm of the City Policy Board, is conceived as an expert unit, operating to advise the board on budgetary and economic issues. Attached neither to the central service-delivery agencies nor to the local councils—and free to perform the highest-level calculations—this arm of the Policy Board would undertake the following:

—calculate the formulas for district budgets and align these with the central City budget;

—advise the City Policy Board in matters requiring either raising or lowering of the funds for districts or for the central government;

—keep the Policy Board informed of the economic health of the City, because economic strength has a direct bearing on the revenues available;

—determine the revenue estimates, which become the basis for tax levies;

—advise the Policy Board concerning other sources of revenue and the "slanting" of City policy toward other revenues (as, for example, Federal take-over of welfare costs).

The Division of Budget Policy is thus visualized as more than a budget office. It would be an instrument of economic policy, an economic-budgetary research arm, and a fact-finding unit that would

help the City Policy Board resolve budgetary disputes, act as a
mediating arm between the central and the local government agencies
on budgetary matters, and serve as the unit that keeps the revenue-
sharing formulas up-to-date.

Summary and Discussion

Under this proposed budget-making arrangement, the mayoralty
would retain its central Budget Office for the budgetary activities of
all the central agencies and the central City government. The local
districts would have their own budget offices. The City Policy Board
would make the basic budgetary allocation between the district and
central service levels, as well as establish allocations among the
districts.

The reason for the division of authority is clear. A budget office
under the mayor would tend to aggrandize central agencies at the
expense of local ones. A budget office under the Policy Board would
tend to reduce the effectiveness of the mayor as the chief executive
for the whole City. The Task Force therefore proposes that the mayor
retain the central Budget Office, that the local districts be provided
with theirs, and that a budgetary-economic unit be created as an arm
of the Policy Board, advising the Board on all budgetary matters,
creating formulas, making determinations concerning percentage
allocations, counseling on relevant economic matters. The Division
of Budget Policy would provide the board, for the first time, with the
ability to make budgetary decisions with the totality of information
it needs. The board would now become involved in budget preparation.
The City's annual budget would become a visible document.

In this formulation, the major interests of all parties are pre-
served. The mayor is not deprived of his budgetary instruments;
but those instruments are brought under greater scrutiny than they
have been until now. The local districts are assured of fair allocations;
yet they would be constrained by checks and balances against pres-
suring the elected authorities to give them preference over the needs
of the central government.

Alternative Budget-Making Proposals

The Task Force has considered other alternatives. Two of
these are discussed below.

Alternative A

There would be a central City Budget Office, attached to the
mayoralty.

Discussion. This alternative would leave budget preparation in the hands of the mayor. His appointees would put together the central budget and work up the formula percentages and allocations for the local budgets. In effect, budget control, even over the districts, would remain with the mayoralty. The practicalities of power being what they are, the tendency would be to reduce the effectiveness of the districts and to aggrandize the central level of government. In this alternative, the Policy Board and City Council would be left with approval powers, as at present, but with no additional leverage over the budget.

Alternative B

There would be a central City Budget Office, attached to the City Policy Board, rather than the mayoralty.

Discussion. Under this alternative, it has been suggested, there is too substantial a diminution of mayoral power.

On balance, we believe the Task Force's resolution of the conflicting interests is the best possible one.

Other Aspects of Budgeting

Additional District Revenue

The districts should be permitted the privilege of raising additional revenue through receipt of direct grants, fees for services and local licenses, and various small user charges. Eventually, it may be possible to delegate certain direct taxing powers to the districts.

Deployment of Funds

Bulk grants to districts within the allocation formula should be considered as a desirable long-range budgetary objective. The bulk grant would allow flexibility in the local deployment of funds; it would also permit the districts to make choices among the mix of services their residents wish to have delivered. This would lead to a healthy diversity among the districts.

Budget Approval

Budget approval would be a function of the City Council. The Policy Board, having participated in preparation of the budget, would not be involved in the approval process. The Council would have the power to reduce, increase, or alter the budget, as it has at present.

   The City Policy Board would then, within a legally established
period, either accept the council's changes or veto them by majority
vote. The council could over-ride the veto by a two-thirds vote of the
entire body.
   The Task Force recommends that the City Council as well as
the City Policy Board be given the essential, professional budgetary
staff assistance necessary to perform its budget approval function.

Municipal Budgets in the United States

   A study of the budgets of middle-sized U.S. cities reveals the
following information:

City	Population	Annual Budget
Tucson	262,933	$39,106,000
Sacramento	254,413	52,998,000
St. Petersburg	216,232	26,150,000
Tampa	277,767	38,723,000
Des Moines	200,587	37,520,000
Wichita	276,554	61,523,000
Baton Rouge	271,922	39,818,000
Jersey City	260,545	88,389,000
Albuquerque	243,751	44,042,000
Rochester	296,233	157,323,000
Yonkers	204,297	72,529,000
Dayton	243,601	56,730,000

   These figures include expense budget and debt service for capital
expenditures. As the variations indicate, it is not possible closely to
correlate municipal expenditures with service delivery, because of
the many different ways in which services are funded. Moreover,
the figures do not indicate the budgets of municipal services funded by
other than the municipal governments. The figures do, however,
indicate that in the budget plans offered in this report, the proposed
local New York City districts would have sufficient funds to operate
effectively. The funds for individual districts would be within the
parameters of expenditures in middle-sized U.S. cities. These would
not be new funds; the money would devolve from the central budget
for functions transferred to the local governments.

FIGURE 13

Per Capita Municipal Expenditures for Selected Services,
by Population-Size Groups: United States, 1968-69

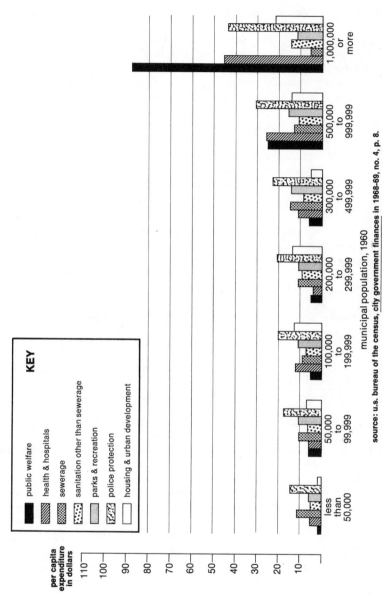

KEY

- ■ public welfare
- ▨ health & hospitals
- ▨ sewerage
- ⦂ sanitation other than sewerage
- ▦ parks & recreation
- ▨ police protection
- ☐ housing & urban development

per capita expenditure in dollars

110 100 90 80 70 60 50 40 30 20 10

less than 50,000 | 50,000 to 99,999 | 100,000 to 199,999 | 200,000 to 299,999 | 300,000 to 499,999 | 500,000 to 999,999 | 1,000,000 or more

municipal population, 1960

source: u.s. bureau of the census, city government finances in 1968-69, no. 4, p. 8.

large cities must cope with those services which, in the main, are least amenable to economies of scale. with certain notable exceptions, per capita cost of municipal service delivery rise sharply after the 300,000 population figure is reached.

67

THE CITY ADMINISTRATOR'S OFFICE

The Task Force recommends rehabilitation and strengthening
of the City Administrator's Office. Transfer of the management
function to the Budget Bureau has been proposed, but we consider
such a transfer to be regressive, in that it would subordinate management to budget.

Improved administration is a primary need in City government.
Concern about the deterioration of administration has been expressed
to the Task Force by management people, by union leaders, and by
witnesses who complain about the failures of service delivery.

Government administration is a complex matter, requiring the
utilization not only of the traditional techniques but of a variety of
new ones, from management reporting systems to operations research.
Both the central agencies and the local districts will need management assistance. Moreover, there may be occasions when a local
district function may need to be temporarily superseded. Qualified
technicians should always be available for this purpose.

The City Administrator's Office has been weakened in recent
years; in fact, it never attained the vitality originally contemplated
for it. The reason is that mayors have been able to use it for whatever purpose they wish. The City Administrator's Office should become what it was originally intended to be—the major managerial
instrument of municipal government. It should perform continuing
studies for the improvement of governmental operations. It should
be the management firefighter, ready to jump in when something is
going wrong in either a central-level or a local-level agency, diagnose
the difficulty, and suggest remedies. It should be the governmental
agency that sets up new departments as needed and liquidates those
that have outlived their usefulness—doing so, though, with the approval
of the City Policy Board. It should examine management techniques
used elsewhere in the world that could be applicable in New York
City. The agency should be empowered to initiate studies on its own,
as well as to accept requests for assistance from district councils.

Among its duties, the City Administrator's Office could take on
the responsibility of advising the City Policy Board concerning the
movement of municipal functions between the two tiers, as experience
demonstrates the desirability of such movement; of recommending the
establishment of new services; and of providing managerial services,
optionally, to the local districts.

In sum, the office must perform a continuing function having
three parts—the sponsorship of management planning, the monitoring
of operations, the evaluation of services performed. Since we have
proposed placing genuine executive power in each of two tiers of

government, we must provide this planning-monitoring-evaluation resource for each tier. The resource should be available to both tiers in a manner effective for the solution of administrative problems. Yet the very act of providing such a resource creates an organizational problem. Where should the management unit be placed? With the mayor? With the City Policy Board? In either case, serious problems would be inevitable. If the unit remains an arm of the mayor, the county executive facing administrative problems would be put in a position of dependency on the mayor for the staff to research and resolve them. If the office were an arm of the Policy Board, the mayor's power would be somewhat diminished. But he would still be in a dominant position since he is the Board's chairman.

One possible solution would be to do what has been proposed in the cases of budget and of planning: create a small staff of management experts to operate under the Policy Board, which would be available to the board and to the districts, and leave the City Administrator's Office under the mayor.

There are shortcomings to this proposal. The techniques of administration are the same, whether applied to the central level or to the district level. The creation of two staffs would involve duplication and possible competition. Moreover, in advising public authorities concerning the movement of functions and services between the governmental tiers, the City Administrator's Office would need to survey both local and central operations.

The Task Force believes that ultimately the City Administrator's Office should be placed under the City Policy Board. We recognize, however, the concern of those who are accustomed to the strong-mayor concept that any such transfer would hamper the mayor in the performance of his functions.

In this case, because of the importance of the City Administrator's Office, and the desirability of revitalizing it, the Task Force has deferred a firm conclusion as to what should be done.

Perhaps the problem would solve itself during the transition period. For during the transition, management services of the kind delivered by a City Administrator's Office would plainly be required by the Transition Task Force (see Chapter 6). And for practical purposes, the bulk of the City Administrator's Office would be working with the transition group. During that period, the office should develop a strength and integrity which would enable it to function effectively no matter where it is eventually placed in the reorganized structure.

PLANNING

Planning would be a function shared by the central and local levels. The key to success in such a shared relationship is a clear definition of the roles that central and local planners are to perform.

In New York City's present planning structure, the City Planning Commission and the local community boards each theoretically passes on the same project; in reality, though, the City Planning Commission has all the power, the local planning boards none. That is a formula for chaos.

Under the proposed structure, each level would have a clearly defined jurisdiction, with as little overlap as possible. In any case of overlapping, the City Policy Board would resolve the matter.

The Task Force has not as yet completed its analysis of the planning function. A detailed report on the subject is in preparation. Nevertheless, the appropriate areas of activity of the two planning levels are, at this writing, clear in broad outline.

The Central Planning Function

There is an initial question: who should be in charge of central planning? Until the 1961 Charter was adopted, planning was the function of an independent mayoral-appointed agency, the City Planning Commission. The results were unsatisfactory.

Under the 1961 Charter, the Planning Department became a mayoral agency, headed by the chairman of the City Planning Commission, which survived as a sort of semi-independent appendix to the Planning Department. Planning became a mayoral function. Again, the results have not been satisfactory.

We have resisted the temptation to find some other place for the planning function. Rather, we have attempted to redefine the central planning function so as to eliminate those aspects of planning that are properly local, and to redefine the local planning role so as to prevent interference with what are properly central planning functions.

The Task Force recommends that the Planning Department remain a central agency operating wholly under the mayor. Its decisions, however, would require Policy Board approval, just as the City Planning Commission's decisions now require Board of Estimate approval. The Policy Board would have its own small division of planning to assist its members in reaching informed judgments.

The Task Force has considered the role of the City Planning Commission. Is it a necessary body? Is its function indispensible as an overlay upon the work of the Planning Department? We

recommend that the City Planning Commission be abolished, on the
grounds that it has not performed an indispensible or useful service.
To the extent that it represents a device to facilitate citizen participation in the planning process, that role would be played by the local
districts in a re-structured system.

The central Planning Department would be responsible for
strategic planning, such as the master plan for the whole City, and for
the location of facilities to perform City-wide functions, such as sewage
disposal plants, regional schools, major recreational facilities (Breezy
Point for example), and housing planning. Close cooperation would
be maintained with existing regional and national agencies.

The central Planning Department would not have exclusive
jurisdiction for all planning. But it would have the predominant voice,
subject to Policy Board approval.

Perhaps the best way to illustrate this as-yet-not-fully-defined
sharing of power is to give an illustration.

We start with the observation that City-wide strategic planning
is not the kind of planning that the City has engaged in for the last
20 years. It has rather, performed basically local planning from a
central level. The 1971 Forest Hills housing situation is a prime
example.

Let us assume under our proposal that the City determines,
as a matter of policy, that it is desirable to create new housing for
the aged and for lower-income people and to locate that housing in
more affluent surroundings. A proper form of City-wide strategic
planning would involve analysis of all the City's neighborhoods (or
the local districts, if the Task Force plan were in effect) and determination of those that have substantial under-representation of aged
and low-income residents. The Planning Department may determine,
for example, that of 35 districts in the City, 22 are in this category.

The Planning Department would thereupon formulate a program
that would allocate a given number of housing units for aged and lower-
income residents to the 22 more affluent districts.

Like all Planning Department decisions, the proposal would
require approval by the City Policy Board. Once approved, there
would be a City-wide program allocating a given number of low-income
families to each of the more affluent districts.

The Local Planning Function

At that point, the local districts would take over. Each of them
would, through their local departments of planning and their local
councils, in consultation with the City Planning Department, determine
the sites for the new housing, whether the units would be high-rise or

low-rise, concentrated or scattered, in new buildings or rehabilitated old ones, and the architectural style. There would be a limit on the length of time that could be spent on site selection, in order to prevent delaying of projects indefinitely by foot-dragging; if the local districts did not act in time, the central government could act for them.

In this relationship, a strategic plan would be formulated by the central Planning Department and approved by the Policy Board. Implementation of the plan would become a local function in which the local community has a voice. But the local community could not simply say "No! We want no low-income people in our district."

There would be similar shared jurisdiction for all clearly City-wide strategic plans. As soon as the City Planning Department reached a tentative decision to locate some central City facility within a particular district, the department would be required to discuss the matter with the appropriate county executive and the officials of the local district affected. Since the project would require approval of the City Policy Board, the county executive in such circumstances would necessarily act as an arbiter: if the facility were needed in the City, or specifically in his borough, he would find it extremely difficult simply to be negative. At the same time, the local reactions could be ascertained long before any kind of final decision were made. Negotiation and accommodation would necessarily occur. They are better instruments than confrontation. They would occur early, not late.

Site selection would be a shared central-local function. Thus, while the City Planning Department, as part of a strategic plan, may propose the location of a housing project, high school, library, recreational center, or some other central facility in a particular district, actual selection of the site should be the district's prerogative. The only limitations on such site selection privileges should be a rule permitting the City Planning Department, with Policy Board approval, to veto the location of a project if it is within a given distance of the district's boundaries, if the site impinges on any other public use, or if it is inconsistent with overall City-wide planning policy.

Each district would have its local planning officer and a small staff, drawn initially from the present Planning Department. The local planning staff would be the arm of the district government in its dealings with the City Planning Department. The local planning staff would make recommendations to the local council on site selection, architectural style, and local implementation concerning City-wide policies.

Each district would have a flat capital budget allocation each year for such local projects as district parks, recreation centers, replacement of street lights, and other capital projects established by the district in order of priority; the planning for these amenities

would also be done locally. In addition, the local planning staff would
have the power to initiate projects which would cost more than the
flat capital budget allowance. These projects would be submitted
through the district executive and local council for possible inclusion
in the capital budget.

Each district's planning department should also be advised by a
community board drawn from the citizenry of the district, generally
comparable to the present community boards appointed by the borough
presidents. Perhaps the community board itself would serve in this
capacity.

The Capital Budget

The City Planning Department would formulate that portion
of the City's capital budget which relates to central City projects.
Local districts would formulate their own capital budgets and submit
them to the county executives of their boroughs. It would be the function of the City Policy Board to make the ultimate determinations as
to which projects are to be included and as to what proportion of the
capital budget (in excess of a flat allowance to each district) should
be allocated to local projects and what proportion to the central City's
projects. In doing this, the Policy Board would have the assistance
of its own planning and budget staffs, as well as the local and central
planning departments.

The Task Force makes clear its recognition of the predominance
of central strategic planning. But the central level planners must
leave the local details to be filled in within the framework of the central
plan by those locally responsible.

Zoning

Zoning, like planning, would be a shared function. The principal
zoning responsibility would be vested in the central governmental
level. But the districts have a significant role to play. That relationship—and the details of the local district's role in planning generally—
will be spelled out in a future report of the Task Force.

POLICE

We regard the present breakdown in public safety as posing
the most critical threat to the life of New York City. However, we
do not recommend attempting to solve the public safety problem by
decentralizing the Police Department.

The creation of local districts would, though, inevitably lead to a demand by citizens for the districts to take action in an effort to maintain and increase the safety of the neighborhoods that each district would encompass.

If local districts are created and are denied the right to play a role in the maintenance of safety, we are concerned that some citizens may take action outside the structure of government and that the wave of lawlessness that has swept the City would be matched by a wave of equally lawless vigilantism.

The desire of citizens to protect their homes and neighborhoods is a legitimate one, and government must facilitate a legitimate implementation of that legitimate desire.

In response to the crime problem, many have urged the localizing of certain police functions, such as street patrol. We conclude, however, especially in light of the presently ongoing efforts to revitalize and localize police services, that it is preferable to preserve unified overall control of that sensitive department. The freedom to deploy police manpower swiftly, and in whatever numbers needed, to any part of the City, counsels in the direction of retaining the Police Department as a central agency.

Critical to this determination is the recommendation that local districts be authorized, under police direction and control, to supplement police services with local residents, private guards, and other appropriate means, at least until the current wave of lawlessness and violence in New York City is brought under control.*

We therefore recommend that the police function should remain under the mayor as a central function. The precinct lines, however, should be harmonized with the new local district lines, and local commanders should be directed to establish close working relations with the local district authorities. In assignment policies, the police should be mandated to make an effort to assign policemen to precincts in which they live or as close to their homes as possible. The archaic three-platoon rule should be abolished, and commanders should be given authority to deploy their troops as they deem best. The steps now being taken to localize police command should be encouraged.

---

*A significant research into supplementary police service has been conducted by two Harvard University faculty members, Gary T. Marx and Dane Archer. Entitled "Citizen Involvement in the Law Enforcement Process," their paper appears in American Behavioral Scientist, XV, 1 (September-October 1971). The authors conclude: "There is clearly a need for citizen efforts [in local community policing], and it becomes increasingly important to understand them."

PUBLIC AND QUASI-PUBLIC
AGENCIES

An unfinished aspect of the Task Force's work involves the
various Model Cities offices and councils, community corporations,
other anti-poverty organizations, and community service agencies
now funded jointly by the Federal government and the City government.
In addition, there are more than 250 voluntary agencies operating programs financed by public funds under contract with community corporations. All of these organizations deal with local social and economic
problems of the kind that could be more effectively administered or
coordinated by community district governments.

At the present time, there is a proliferation of these community
service agencies; this often results in duplication of programs and
lack of overall coordination. It makes sense to the Task Force to
recommend eventually bringing such agencies, including their programs and budgets, under the jurisdiction of the local community
district governments.

The Task Force is completing a separate report on these agencies
and on the related Federal-State-local relationships. (A study of
Federal funding of certain of these agencies appears as an appendix
to this report.)

CIVIL SERVICE AND COLLECTIVE
BARGAINING

In a two-level governmental structure, both collective bargaining
and civil service recruitment and examination should remain central.
The local districts would have neither the power nor the expertise
to deal with the complex matters of labor relations and the intricate
interweaving of law, procedure, regulations, and union agreements
that constitutes the basis of working conditions in government. Moreover, it would make little sense, even if it were possible, to have
different pay scales and different conditions of work in the various
districts. The result would be continuous wage "leap-frogging" and
"whiplashing", as unions sought to play district against district.

In a re-structured system, the merit system would remain the
basis of public employment, both for the central and local governmental
tiers. Central agencies would hire from civil service lists, as at
present. Districts would also hire from centrally-established civil
service lists; the same lists would be utilized for similar or related
services. Where necessary, separate lists for special district needs
would be established, as they are today for specialized departmental

needs. We suggest, however, that each district be afforded, within existing service regulations and requirements, the right to give preference to its own residents who fully meet the job qualifications.

The suggestion has been made that City-wide contract negotiations be limited to wages, hours, and working conditions, grievance procedures, seniority provisions, and arbitration of disputes. While collective bargaining on these subjects would remain central, the day-to-day matters of personnel relationships should be local, since the person working for a district government will be that district's employee. The supervisor must have a role in judging the job-performance of those under his supervision. Obviously, the district must be able to apply disciplinary measures to an employee whose work is unsatisfactory. In order adequately to perform its assigned functions, each district must also have some control over the deployment of personnel, work rules, and employee transfer.

Civil service labor relations, the prerogatives of employee organizations and the limits of their inroads into management, the right of local governments to function at maximum possible efficiency and to seek maximum employee productivity, the question of what subjects are proper for collective bargaining and what are not—these questions must be openly and courageously faced by all levels of government and by the employee representatives. These questions have remained gray areas for too long. The interest of the City's people, the economic stability of the City government (whether or not decentralized), the defense of the merit system, and ultimately the protection of the employees themselves—these require a forthright, honest examination of this area.

The Task Force's advisors on public personnel policy perceive no serious problems arising from the centralizing of the qualification and bargaining processes; the localizing of parts of the personnel administration process, including the local hiring of people found qualified by the central qualifying body; and pay scales established by centralized bargaining.

To the extent possible, rigidities of the ranking system should be reduced, and the prohibitions against lateral entry into the service should be relaxed. These changes would have the result of opening up opportunities to larger numbers of those who have shown themselves qualified by achieving satisfactory civil service ratings. Relaxing strict adherence to the ranking system would also reduce the chances of unfair discrimination, particularly against members of minority groups. Recent Federal court decisions, finding certain tests and job qualifications discriminatory, reinforce the concept that the ranking system be made more flexible.

There will be need for middle-management supervisory personnel in the districts. We recommend that these positions be opened up, on

a first choice basis, as promotion opportunities to present qualified
civil service employees. These employees constitute an important
pool of talent.

Civil Service Academy

One of the first tasks in the transition is the training and upgrading of the present civil service employees to assume middle-
management roles. This is essential both for the central government
and for the new local governments. The reservoir of middle-management employees in the City service is rapidly diminishing, as those
who entered civil service in the 1930s and the 1940s are retiring.
The Task Force has been given information that within two years a
major gap is likely, as these trained echelons leave and are not replaced.

The Task Force recommends the swift establishment of a civil
service training and employee upgrading facility. Training programs,
arranged by the Department of Personnel with the universities, in
cooperation with the unions, should prepare qualified employees to
take over middle-management supervisory positions. One great
advantage would accrue from using the available talent pool: these
employees know the City.

THE CITY'S COMMAND DECENTRALIZATION
PLAN

The Task Force examined a number of models of decentralization—the "command decentralization" plan of the City government, as well as the plans prepared by the Borough Presidents of Manhattan, the Bronx, Brooklyn, Staten Island and Queens, and the plans of other cities, both American and foreign, which operate on more than one level. All of these plan have something to contribute to the final proposal that we recommend the City adopt. And all have contributed to the proposal advanced by the Task Force. We have borrowed freely and we acknowledge our debt.

On January 14, 1972, the City administration began an experiment in what it calls command decentralization, setting up local centers in five community districts in an effort to achieve coordination among basic services. An additional objective is to develop information systems concerning local service delivery. Long-range, the City Office of Neighborhood Government hopes to establish similar operations in some 60 areas, which would be approximately coextensive with the present 62 community planning districts.

We regard the City's experiment as useful evidence that it is possible to create multi-purpose governmental districts that can deliver a multitude of services within common local boundaries, notwithstanding the incredible complexity and lack of similarity in the existing service districts. The experiment may also furnish helpful experience and information to the body that would have to be created in order to make a transition from single-level to two-level government.

Nevertheless, there are four specific aspects of the City's decentralization model that lead us to conclude the plan cannot achieve all the results claimed for it:

First, the attempt to shift decision-making to a lower level within the same administrative hierarchy could be described as "unnatural," since the natural tendency of any hierarchy, as Professor Alan K. Campbell has pointed out, is to shift upward, not downward, the power to make decisions. Any experiment seeking to reverse that natural trend can work only temporarily and only in selected special experimental areas, and affects only those decisions regarded by superiors in the hierarchy as being of relatively limited importance.

Second, the City's program includes no counterforce, in the form of locally based citizen input, to this upward bureaucratic flow of power. For the City's plan omits any provision for citizen participation. While the Task Force does not accept much of the rhetoric surrounding the idea of "community control," we do recognize and give great weight to the importance of allowing the citizens of a given area to fix their own local priorities and to hold their own municipal employees accountable.

Given a choice between supervision of the delivery of local services by a staff of centrally-appointed officials and supervision by a locally-based and locally responsible elected official, we opt for the latter. It would be more responsive and more satisfying to the citizen, and possibly more efficient and less expensive as well.

Third, we regard the City's proposal as unlikely to result in any unification of services at the local level. The City has provided for a local manager in each of its experimental districts, but the manager has no power to manage at all; he is no more than a local complaint bureau or expediter. This, it seems to us, is a basic flaw in the City's program. Under the plan, the local manager's decisions are all subject to central review. He has little budget to work with. His only power of coordination lies in his personal ability to persuade local service chiefs to cooperate with him. The plan carefully sidesteps any experimentation with new fiscal or budgetary approaches. Unless the local superintendents of services voluntarily acquiesce to the suggestions of the manager, the problem must be referred up the hierarchy to the appropriate commissioner or administrator level for resolution—thus going up two hierarchial levels instead of one.

Fourth, the City's proposal will create another obstacle to the accomplishment of what the City professes to be the final step in its program—"political decentralization." The creation of a number of new local administrative structures will result in yet another centralized bureaucracy of supervisors who can be expected to resist the transfer of local political power from the central appointed City administrators to locally elected officials.

Indeed, in one respect at least, the mistakes of the initial school decentralization experiment are being repeated in the City's command decentralization plan. In the initial school decentralization experiment, four local boards were created, but, as the City pointed out, "the essence of power remained in the central bureaucracies." A clash was inevitable, and it took place. To avoid such a clash in its command decentralization plan, the City has done one thing and avoided doing another: it has created a local bureaucracy as a branch and subordinate part of the central bureaucracy; it has denied participation to the residents of the pilot areas.

If local participation should eventually arrive, a clash between locally elected boards and the established local administrators would perhaps be just as troublesome as it was in the school decentralization experiment. Possibly more so, because the central bureaucracy would have its own people in the district, busy running things under central control and hostile to the intrusion of new masters.

THE TRANSITION

How would the transition to district governments take place?

Precedents

A form of transition occurred in 1962, when administrative functions were removed from the borough presidents and transferred to the mayoralty. The changeover proceeded with such smoothness that the ripples were hardly felt. The transition involved the creation of new agencies; the dismantling, transfer, and re-assembling of equipment; the acquisiton of new shop and office space; the shifting of employees from former jobs to positions within the mayor's jurisdiction. The task was one involving much detail and requiring sensitivity to the needs of public employees. It was carried out by a team from the City Administrator's Office, with the cooperation of other municipal services.

We have examined reorganizations in other major cities, and we find that they, too, occur without undue disruption of services, provided they are done with care and adequate time.

If the lessons gained from these transition-to-decentralization experiences are properly heeded, if careful planning and implementation are carried out, if sufficient time is allowed so that the new districts can be set up at their own pace—then the transition to a two-level system in New York City can be accomplished without major disruptions.

Preconditions for the Transition

The transition should be carried out with care and without rushing.
Certain preconditions are clearly essential:
—The district borders must be delineated.
—Service, power, and function allocations between the tiers must
be determined.
—The rights and privileges of public employees must be protected,
and these public employees must be assured first choice of the newly
created jobs. As a general rule, as the jobs go from one tier to another, the employees go with them. Intensive training programs
should be instituted in order to build up a middle management corps.
—Proper budgetary arrangements must be made.
—Districts should not be compelled to set up fully operating
local governments until ready to do so. Some districts would be able
to assume governmental powers almost at once; others would perhaps
take several years until they were ready. The key to smooth transition
is allowing sufficient time and planning with the newly elected officials.
—Essential to successful transition in New York City would be
election of the new local governments at least a year before they would
begin to exercise power, so that the newly elected officials could play
a major role in creating their own bureaucracies. They should have
a major voice in selecting from the existing centralized agencies
those individuals who will head up the services in the new local areas.
In making such allocations, it is essential that the central City employees be assigned to new districts that are more than lines on a
map.
—Preparations for the transition would have to involve pains-
taking study of personnel and functions in the existing City work force,
as well as careful analysis of the personnel needs of each district in
light of the population mix and physical size. It would require flexibility to protect employees of the City from being left without any
employing agency. Some employees may have to be the beneficiaries
of so-called "grandfather" clauses and be continued in employment
until retirement although no real need for their jobs would exist.

Transition Task Force

A special unit—the Transition Task Force—should be created
to carry out the details of changeover. This team, consisting of
highly-qualified administrators, budget experts, management technicians, and legal personnel, would undertake to do the detail work
involved. The team, which might be chosen partially from existing

agencies, should be disengaged from all other duties during the period of transition.*

A legal group would need to begin preparation, after the charter is completed, of the more detailed administrative code.

Information assembled by the Office of Neighborhood Government and other City agencies in their efforts to establish and evaluate the present program for command decentralization should be made available to the Transition Task Force.

A basic for administrative decentralization already exists in the form of the many service districts. They are today neither coordinated nor responsive to local situations. However, with the alignment of service districts and the new local districts, readymade local administrative cadres would be available.

Community planning boards, other quasi-governmental local agencies, and civic groups provide a nucleus of personnel for elective office under political decentralization.

Concerns about the Transition

The concern is sometimes expressed that transition to a two-level governmental system would be insuperably difficult and costly. We do not dismiss such concerns as irrelevant, but emphasize that transition, while not easy, is manageable and is necessary to achieve meaningful reform.

Another expressed concern is that the new communities would not be able to govern themselves. Such fears fail to consider a simple fact: new U.S. communities continue to be organized constantly, as they have been since the beginning of colonial history. They are organized today, as new towns and new suburban communities come into being. They are organized under State laws and with the ongoing participation of new residents. They are organized usually without major stress and strain. There is no reason to believe that New Yorkers would be any less capable of organizing themselves into politically viable communities. Probably the reverse is true.

New Yorkers have a long tradition of political know-how. They have civic and quasi-governmental organizations that are immensely knowledgeable, and the newer community groups have proven articulate and capable. The essential legal and technical expertise is available

---

*The essential working staff could be assembled from the personnel of the following existing agencies: City Administrator's Office, Budget Bureau, Municipal Service Administration, Department of Personnel.

in New York City as nowhere else; in fact, it is an expertise that the City actually exports, as its public administration experts travel throughout the world assisting other cities to organize and reorganize themselves.

It is clear, therefore, that the time is long overdue to lay to rest that ancient canard about New Yorkers being unable to govern themselves.

Cost of Transition

The costs involved in transition cannot all be added up on an accountant's ledger. Despite widely expressed assertions that the re-structure would be immensely costly, no evidence supports such statements. The costs would not cause overwhelming impact upon the municipal budget. The City now has more than 2,000 municipal shops and offices scattered throughout the five boroughs. Many of these would become available for immediate use by the new local districts, either singly or jointly. They would not in every case be ideally situated, but they would be there. Thus, no vast new capital construction would be immediately required for district government buildings. Where necessary, additional structures should be leased during the early years of transition.

The changeover of services and functions from central to local control would involve the transfer of employees, not additional employees. The ratio of public employees per 10,000 citizens is higher in New York City than in any other municipality. It is the Task Force's considered opinion that most of the new positions could be filled by existing personnel and within existing budgetary allocations. With reasonable union cooperation, there need be no great problem in the transfer of employees from one jurisdiction to another; the employees' legitimate rights and privileges would be protected. In fact, the necessity for district middle management would open up new promotional opportunities for the present corps of civil servants.

We visualize no vast additional salary cost. There is even reason to believe that elements of lower cost may be foreseen. As services devolve from the central City to the district tiers, the number of employees at the central tier would be reduced.* Moreover,

---

*The London reorganization experience demonstrates a lowering of central government budget after reorganization. A research study issued by the Royal Commission on Local Government in England and dealing with the financial effects of reorganization pointed out that,

district, government, which implies more visible government, should
lead to increased employee productivity and reduction of waste, because
local citizens would be more acutely aware than they are now of who
their employees are and what these employees are doing where and
when—and how well.

Some service costs may increase because of new demands and
new government programs. These costs would be increased whether
government is decentralized or not. One example may be given.
There is a growing attitude that aged residents ought not to be cast
out, ought not to be treated as unwanted derelicts. Simple humanity
demands greater governmental sensitivity to the needs of the aged,
and pressures are building up in the direction. One service that surely
could better be accomplished locally would be care of the aged, and
there would, of course, be cost factors involved.

Certain services could be purchased by local districts for less
money than those services cost by traditional governmental methods.
Flexibility should be permitted. If a local district can prune trees
in its parks for less money, or can get its motor vehicles repaired
more cheaply, or can purchase garbage pickup for less than the cost
now imposed, it should have the right to do so. The money saved could
be used either to reduce budget or to pay for other services that the
local district may wish to undertake. There would thus be a built-in
incentive to get services performed in a less expensive, not the most
expensive way.

The expense of a part-time elected council, the elections themselves, a local executive and a staff, the local district centers, and
local service facilities would be virtually the only new costs. Their
impact on the City budget would be relatively small, less than the
savings resulting from abolition of the City's super-agencies. Most
other costs, under rigorous control, would devolve down from their
present lines in the City budget.

------

at the local level, there were some increased costs "due to the levelling
up or raising of standards . . . but the majority of people would regard
this as desirable. . . . On the other hand, the findings of a team of
Borough Treasurers . . . suggests that the increase in expenditure
inside London and in the county boroughs outside the city was not
very different. . . . The greater part of the increase (the Treasurers
said) is thus due to factors affecting the country as a whole rather
than to the London reforms." See Greater London Group, the London
School of Economics, Lessons of the London Government Reforms
(London: Her Majesty's Stationery Office, 1968).

Moreover, if it were to become possible for the local districts to supervise budgets of the many quasi-governmental agencies—such as community corporations and poverty agencies, which are now operating almost independently—an increase in the effectiveness with which those funds are used could well be anticipated.

Summary

What, then, are the steps to be taken, after establishment of a charter revision commission*, after the drafting of a charter mandating a two-level system of government, and after adoption of the charter by the people in referendum? The tasks, all of which would proceed concurrently under the Transition Task Force on the basis of clear timetables, are:

1. Examination of all laws, rules, and regulations affected by the new charter.

2. Drafting of a new administrative code, which would contain the details of governance.

3. Establishment of district lines.

4. Alignment of service-delivery districts so that they are co-extensive with the local districts.

5. Preparation of an inventory of all services delivered to the residents of the City, together with an inventory of the employees who deliver these services.

6. Activation of new budget machinery.

7. Allocations of services, functions, budget, power, and personnel and equipment to the newly designated levels of government.

8. Preparation of district council elections.

9. Administrative assistance to the districts in setting up their governmental structures; assignment of a provisional district manager to each local district to begin organizing the district under the new plan.

10. Reorganization of agencies in the central tier.

---

*In May 1972, the New York State Legislature enacted a measure (S. 10475) in relation to the establishment of temporary state charter commissions for cities in the state.

While this report basically deals with the decentralization of New York City's government, the Task Force is well aware that any re-structuring of municipal functions must consider regional aspects as well.

In its deliberations, the Task Force has considered the basic question of U.S. federalism. At what levels do the various governmental functions, services, and powers properly belong? What should a City's functions be? Must the same governmental unit that pays for services also be the one that raises the revenues or delivers the services? Might not income maintenance services for the poor be better delivered for being financed by the Federal government and administered by State and local governments?

INTERDEPENDENCE

Clearly, some functions—among them transportation, air and water pollution control, water supply, and waste disposal—cannot be handled effectively by any individual community, not even one as large as New York City. These are functions that affect a region and that, to be administered adequately, require governmental jurisdictions broader than the City's. Clearly, too, the economy of New York City is intimately related to that of its contiguous neighbors. There are significant economic and social costs and benefits that spill over from New York City into the surrounding areas, as well as from the surrounding areas into the City. For example, the benefits of the City's outstanding cultural resources spill over into the surrounding communities, which are able to take advantage of these cultural opportunities. The benefits represented by large pools of skilled

manpower in the suburban counties are shared by employers in the
City. A reverse manpower movement—City to suburb—is also evident.

In the same manner, social and economic costs also spill over
from the City into the surrounding areas and from the surrounding
areas into the City. For example, the effects of air pollution, drug
addiction, crime and segregated housing practices in one community
spill over into neighboring communities.*

Throughout the United States and the rest of the world, new
governmental and administrative mechanisms are being devised to
deal with problems of metropolitan responsibility and the distribution
of services in larger-than-city areas. A report by the Committee
for Economic Development has stated the matter succinctly: "All
metropolitan areas are affected to a greater or lesser extent by the
conflicting forces of centralization and decentralization. The inter-
dependence of activities within metropolitan areas requires area-wide
institutions for some functions or parts of functions of government.
Just as clear is the need for units of government small enough to
enable the recipients of government services to have some voice and
control over their quality and quantity."[7]

In the New York-New Jersey-Connecticut region, regional
matters are dealt with in a variety of ways: by regional authorities,
such as the Port Authority of New York and New Jersey and the
Metropolitan Transportation Authority; by specialized entities, such
as the Tri-State Regional Planning Commission and the Interstate
Sanitation Commission; by local, voluntary inter-governmental bodies,
such as the Metropolitan Regional Council; and through haphazard,
uncoordinated, and occasional inter-governmental cooperation.

---

*One method of dealing with the spillover problem involving
fiscal inequities has been initiated in the seven-county metropolitan
area centered on Minneapolis-St. Paul, Minnesota. The Minnesota
State Legislature adopted a plan in 1971 that provides for a metropoli-
tan-wide pooling of 40 percent of all net growth in the industrial and
commercial property tax base after 1971. Each community then
receives back an assigned share of this pooled revenue, the share
being determined basically by population size but being adjusted so
that communities with lower-than-average property valuation receive
a larger proportion, while communities with greater revenue capacity
get back a proportionately smaller share. This system enables each
community in the metropolitan area to benefit from commercial or
industrial growth even though that growth does not occur within the
community's own boundaries. Communities where commercial growth
is impractical or undesirable are thus not penalized so much for
their lack. See Citizens League News, XX, 12 (July 1971).

A better approach to regionalism must come. The Task Force believes the three states which comprise this region have a stake in the creation of more adequate regional mechanisms. We propose that New York State invite New Jersey and Connecticut to work jointly toward such mechanisms. And, in the proposals we are making for re-structuring the government of New York City, we are leaving major units open-ended so that in time these may cooperate more effectively with their neighbor governments in approaching regional problems, or may eventually form basic units of regional entities.

RE-STRUCTURING CITY GOVERNMENT IS A
FIRST PRIORITY

For a number of reasons, however, we have not attempted in this report to make specific recommendations for regional mechanisms to deal with Greater New York's region-wide problems.

First, we believe there is a degree of urgency in dealing with the internal structural problems of the City. It is our contention that the proposals in this report for decentralizing government will substantially increase the City's capacity to handle its own problems and therefore they should be implemented without delay.

Second, the Task Force is still in the process of exploring which services are best provided within a regional jurisdiction, which mechanisms are most appropriate for planning and delivering those services, and what the impact of these mechanisms would be. We are not yet certain whether new governmental or quasi-governmental units are needed, or whether existing regional units could be adapted to serve broader purposes. These and other matters are now under study.

Third, while it is feasible to arrive at more rational regional jurisdictions than presently exist, we detect a substantial reluctance on the part of New York City's neighbors toward the creation of a strong regional entity. We do not believe it is politically feasible to persuade New York City's neighboring counties and states to join in a regional government at the present time. Many of New York City's neighbors fear the City and what appear to them as its insurmountable problems. We believe that our plan of re-structure, when adopted and implemented, will go a long way toward enabling the City to cope better with its problems, thus creating the kind of political climate that will make broader regional government possible.

The Task Force is currently at work on a group of reports dealing with various aspects of the region—functions that could be reallocated regionally, as well as with approaches for cooperative

arrangements among the communities of the region, the State of New
York and its neighboring states, and the Federal government.

THE CONCEPT OF MULTIPLE REGIONS

One of the ideas the Task Force is examining involves abandoning
the theoretical construct of a single region. The "region" would be
replaced by a design of multiple regions within the tri-state area,
each of them flexible and each of them interlocking functionally with
the others. The separate regions would not necessarily be spatially
co-extensive. In such a context, for example, the water pollution
region would involve portions of the three states abutting the major
waterways, extending a substantial distance up the Hudson beyond
Poughkeepsie and including the New York and Connecticut sides of
Long Island Sound. The air pollution region would involve another
area—all of New York City, Nassau County, and the industrial tier
of northeastern New Jersey. The water supply region would extend
to the sources of the City's water supply, including all the areas along
its water supply pipelines and reservoirs, and all of Long Island.
The transportation region would have still different boundaries,
extending fingers into the three states, beyond Princeton, New Jersey,
beyond Bridgeport, Connecticut, and as far east into Suffolk County
as the daily commuter journey-to-work.
Other functions would require other regional borders. These
borders would necessarily be flexible, as development, technology,
and migration movement entail changes.
Recent history indicates that this concept of multiple regions
may be more acceptable than the single-region concept that has been
pressed for the past 20 years—but the acceptance of which has been
fiercely resisted in the suburban areas.
Two other suggestions are interrelated with the multiple-region
concept.
The first of these is the requirement for a coordinating regional
mechanism. The Task Force is examining the possibility of putting
together such existing groups as the Tri-State Regional Planning
Agency and the Metropolitan Regional Council, and making a place
in this arrangement for the effective but private Regional Plan Association. This approach may involve a coordinating group consisting of
local, State, and Federal officials. But no definite conclusions have yet
been reached. The study of such a coordinating mechanism involves
the comparative analysis of comparable agencies in other parts of
the United States and in Europe.
The second suggestion concerns the requirement that certain
municipal functions move into a regional framework. City-wide

planning ought to fit into a wider, regional planning scheme. Housing problems in the City cannot be solved without also considering how suburban housing is financed and how it is related to City population and density.

Still other questions remain to be considered and answered. Among them: How should regional entities be financed? What feasible alternatives are there to insulated decision-making by public authorities? Should a metropolitan entity be responsible for performing both planning and service delivery, or should these functions be handled separately? How should representation be allocated in a federated metropolitan system? How should regional planning be coordinated with local planning? What systems would be acceptable to all the governments involved?

In presenting the regional questions it is now studying, the Task Force makes clear that it has yet reached no definite conclusions.

8

**OPPOSITION:
SOME QUESTIONS
AND ANSWERS**

Any effort to make a major change in New York City's form of municipal government inevitably encounters resistance. This is particularly true in a change so fundamental as that proposed in this report.

The trend in political science thought in this country during the 20th century has been toward centralism. Authority had to be co-extensive with responsibility, it was argued, if governance was to be effective. The mayor of the City, whoever he may be, was held responsible by the electorate for what happened; therefore, he should have the authority to carry out his responsibility. There was suspicion of the "politicians" and a vague sense that the highest elected official, with his City-wide constituency, somehow stood above political machinations. There was the managerial call for coordination of services; certainly the services needed coordination. Economies of scale were invoked. Benefits of efficiency and cost-savings, it was pointed out, would flow from centralization.

Centralization of executive power, in a degree never before achieved, was written into the 1961 New York City Charter, which became effective in 1963. Although the expected results have not been realized, the proponents of centralization retain an understandable commitment to the idea, since it has been an article of faith so long. They tend to be critical of the reverse concept of political decentralization. A learning period is necessary, as it always is when a radically new and different concept is proposed.

The Task Force's proposal to institute two-level government is a pioneer recommendation. It proposes a rearrangement of governmental powers. We have given serious study to the objections raised. We recognize that they express legitimate concerns. Following are 11 questions that have been most frequently asked, together with our replies.

1. <u>How can you ensure that district governments will hire com-</u>
<u>petent personnel, purchase wisely and economically, and operate</u>
<u>efficiently, avoiding graft and corruption</u>?

We can't guarantee the millenium; neither can we guarantee
government pure, wise, and competent. As for personnel, under our
plan they would come from civil service, tested by merit system
methods, and by the central Department of Personnel. As for purchasing, the local districts would have the option of purchasing from
either the central Department of Purchase, or from other sources if
they wanted to. But if they did purchase elsewhere, it could not be at
a price higher than they would pay the City department, unless they
could adequately justify the action. We see no reason to believe that
New Yorkers working locally would operate less efficiently than New
Yorkers working centrally. The probability is that they would work
more efficiently, because they would be more closely monitored at the
local level, and that there would be little or no "fat" in the budgets—
and no big deal of assistants to assistants.

We can't give any guarantees that there won't be graft and corruption, any more than we could guarantee their absence now in the central
agencies. It is possible, however, to believe that there may be less
corruption, not more, when local functions are locally performed,
locally visible, and more readily monitored. The Task Force plan
also has built in an overview role, which provides that, where there
is dishonesty or gross inefficiency, a local service may be temporarily
superseded.

2. <u>Since one of the objectives of democratic government is broad</u>
<u>participation of citizens in the voting process, and since experience,</u>
<u>both in this country and elsewhere, has shown that only a small</u>
<u>percentage of voters—ranging from perhaps 15 percent to 40 percent</u>
<u>at best—turns out to vote in elections in small districts, how can you</u>
<u>expect any better results in local district council elections in New</u>
<u>York City</u>?

It is never wise to pursue the numbers game in terms of voter
turnout at elections. Such analogies can cut both ways. Those who
make the citations implicit in the question usually point to such things
as poverty board elections in areas where people are crucially involved
in the sheer business of survival. They don't concern themselves with
what might happen in Riverdale, Kew Gardens, or Greenwich Village
if those communities could elect their own councils.

The comparison could as well be made with the 60-75 percent
turn-out in elections in some of the middle-sized cities in the New York
City area, rather than with the low turnout in small special-agency
elections. People in these cities turn out in good numbers because
they have a personal interest and concern in the issues and candidates
being voted on. They believe the candidates they vote for will have

power to carry out the voters' mandates. They think their vote matters. This presupposes that they have read or heard discussions
about the pros and cons of the issues and the merits and weak points
of the candidates.

Wide dissemination of information through the media, plus personal meetings with candidates, are a necessary prerequisite to
bringing people to the polls. This has not been the case in most of the
cited examples, such as the local school board, community corporation,
and poverty board elections in New York City. The poor turnouts in
these cases were due either to a belief that the elections did not mean
much because the persons elected would have little power or to the
fact that the potential voters were uninformed and consequently unin-
terested.

Under the decentralization plan proposed by the Task Force, the
district voters would elect their local district council. Therefore, the
voters would know that the candidate they selected would have power
and also would be functioning in their community, so that they could
hold him or her accountable for performance.

Furthermore, we anticipate that the political parties would be
actively involved in the nomination of candidates for the elective district posts. In order to get nominated and elected, the candidates
would have to make themselves and their platforms known to their
constituencies through personal canvassing, public meetings, and
newspaper, television, and radio interviews. Since it is planned that
district elections would be held on Election Day in November, and that
the candidates would be listed on the regular ballots according to their
political affiliations, the extent of voter participation in the district
elections should be high.

Voting is not the only criterion of participation. People must
have a sense of belonging, of identity with a community, of roots in a
place. And that is one of the objectives of developing small towns
within New York City. Participation involves, in addition to voting,
the capability of going to hearings, joining boards, having somebody
close to home to whom you can complain and make suggestions—and
who has the power and ability to do what is needed.

3. Granted, for the sake of argument, that decentralization is
a concept that should be implemented in New York City, would it not
be desirable to do it gradually, starting with administrative decentralization and proceeding in stages toward political decentralization?

We have been mindful of the admonition to move slowly, we have
weighed the risk-benefit equation, and we have concluded that there is
greater risk in moving too slowly than there is in attempting to move
towards a two-level system of government now, rather than at some
indefinite, unspecified future date. The alternative to excessive speed
is not inaction. Nor is it possible to do the job in bits and pieces.

When one is launching a new structure of government, one must either set sail or stay ashore. We cannot conceive how one can localize a third or quarter of the City and keep the balance on its present single-level centralized basis.

There is, however, a deeper response to this question, in the realm of how power works. Bureaucratic power, once operating in a system of administrative decentralization, will resist enormously every effort to displace it with locally elected people. There is no conceivable gain in taking the route of gradualism and thereby inviting such resistance.

4. Is it wise to change the present structure of City government after less than ten years of experience with the City charter?

Less than ten years is long enough. The overwhelming weight of the testimony presented to the Task Force in its series of public hearings and in conferences with civic leaders and public officials is that New Yorkers are unhappy, frustrated, and disillusioned with the kind of government they have today. The ordinary citizen thinks that "they" down at City Hall "couldn't care less" about his problems and his neighbors'—problems very real to him (and them) such as violence outside and burglaries inside the home; streets that are filthy, congested, and full of potholes; uncollected garbage, unshovelled snow; backed-up sewers; schools where children don't learn; poorly maintained libraries and parks; polluted air; frightening medical bills and fragmented health services; more and more taxes with less and less to show for them. Our public hearings indicate that most New Yorkers, in all five boroughs, think it is time for a change now.

There is nothing in sight to indicate that these conditions will improve under the present structure. Decentralization will not solve all these problems; but it will give the residents of the City a fresh opportunity and new tools to attack the problems of service delivery.

We do not suggest that re-structuring should be undertaken without thought, or without affording the people of the City ample time to consider its implications. After all, the idea of decentralization is not new—most of the proposals we have made are based upon suggestions that have been in the public domain for years. And the demand for re-structuring the City government is sufficiently strong that one cannot merely command it to stop.

5. Won't decentralization into numerous community districts fragment the City?

New York City is fragmented today. The plan we propose would result in the opposite of fragmentation. It would tie together the local entities and the central government in an innovative unity that doesn't exist today. There will still be a strong central mayor. Most services still would be delivered by the central government.

6. Won't a decentralized New York City be ineffectual in bargaining with the State and Federal governments?

In our plan, the mayor is the elected head of the City and the chairman of the City Policy Board. We believe that the City will achieve better results than it does today, in its dealings with the State and Federal governments, when the mayor is able to devote himself more fully to the vital tasks of representing the City's interests in Albany and Washington. He will be relieved of his present preoccupation with the day-to-day crises that arise as long as he is held responsible for every little service breakdown. Also, a study of Federal finding shows that a two-level governmental system will not reduce the flow of governmental grants.

7. Why not start with several experimental districts instead of proceeding directly into City-wide decentralization?

It is impossible to find a "typical" district or two in which to make a test that would produce results valid City-wide. It would be equally impossible to delineate a single test district without creating district lines for an entire borough. If there is general agreement that the decentralization plan has merit, it should be instituted as a totality. The Task Force's findings demonstrate the need for change throughout the City. We build in flexibility. Local districts would proceed at their own pace. And a carefully organized transition will take account of local differences.

8. Won't the costs of operating a two-tier system of government be greater than under the present centralized system?

The steady escalation in the costs of the government we have makes this a problem that must be faced squarely. The overall costs of the two-tier system may be greater, but that is because the costs would go up in any system. When local district councils control the services in their own districts, they and the voters who elect the council members will have a personal stake in seeing that the money they spend yields results in terms of adequate and efficient performance.

We have some reason to believe that costs in a two-tier system may be lower. Here is why. The actual costs of the new governments would have a minimal impact on budget. And because employees would be working closer to the level of citizen visibility (and given reasonable union cooperation), productivity may rise. There is no reason to think that a service delivered locally needs to cost more than the same service delivered centrally.

9. How can you prevent a rise in divisiveness as the more prosperous and knowledgeable districts win out in inevitable competitions for City, State, and Federal grant funds, as well as for the most qualified employees?

Here again the City Policy Board should be able to assist the weaker districts and guide them in learning how to compete with others. If they do this, divisiveness probably would not arise. And, rest assured, the poorer districts will learn.

10. Would districts largely made up of minority groups be able
to govern themselves? Might not militants take over the government
in some of these districts?

The question reveals a distrust of the people. Let us take the
second part of the question first. Suppose "militants" won an election
in Yonkers or in Newark; would that make the winning party ineligible
to take the reins of government in those cities? In a democratic
society, we start by assuming the people have the right to elect whom
they want, no matter who else may or may not like those elected.
Some people fear persons elected as Conservatives or as Liberals
more than they fear "militants." As for "taking over" district governments, there are plenty of legal restraints against that.

Now to the first part of the question. Yes, we feel that districts
made up largely of minority groups would be able to govern themselves.
Minority groups in New York always have. We might add a wry note
here: What bothers New Yorkers is that the present "majority" system
isn't working. Underlying the question is a more basic attitude that
it is the duty of the better, richer, wiser members of society to protect
the less rich, less wise, and less good against their own shortcomings.
In our view, this attitude is about as valid today as it was in the day of
Rudyard Kipling. The British Empire abandoned that piece of snobbery
some time ago, and its former colonies have survived. We suggest it
is time for New Yorkers to abandon it as well.

11. Shouldn't you keep ethnic groups apart in the districts to be
set up? Won't they fight with one another in "mixed" districts and be
unable to govern?

The question is exactly the opposite of the preceding one. Let
us attack it directly, for it, too, reveals a basic distrust of the people.

New York City needs help. Yet suggestions that we learn from
the experience of other cities—especially those outside the United
States—are frequently rejected with a kind of provincial myopia that
insists that somehow American city dwellers are different. We believe
this myopia reflects something more serious and more disturbing—an
elitism that believes that our heterogeneous populations are insuffi-
ciently cohesive to be responsible, that suggests that two-level governments throughout the world have succeeded because they have
homogeneous populations, while we do not. This is really a subtle
demeaning of blacks, Puerto Ricans, and the remnants of earlier im-
migrant groups.

The experience of other major world cities is a useful antidote
to this kind of thinking. Paris has an enormous population of North
Africans. London already has a non-white population of approximately
10 percent. Some of its boroughs have as high as 30 percent nonwhites.
The British approach the problem of population mix pragmatically.
In boroughs of high foreign population, irrespective of ethnic origins,

governmental communications are published in the language used by those who live there, including Urdu, Bengali, Swahili, Greek, and Turkish.

We regard America's diversity as a source of strength, not weakness. That diversity and that strength are reflected in the variety of backgrounds among the groups that make up New York City's population. Indeed, unless these people of diverse backgrounds can work together in local governments to serve their common ends, we are in even more serious trouble than anyone has suggested. For, if the fears of those who distrust the capacities of our diverse populations are well founded, the alternative is some sort of paternal, central government, which "knows best" what is good for the little people down there.

Our present condition demonstrates that the central City government neither knows nor does best. And if current trends continue, New York City will achieve the homogeneity of population that these critics urge, as those who can afford to leave the City do so in increasing numbers. Then they will leave behind a population that does have attributes of homogeneity—a population of the poor and the nonwhite.

Our proposal asks the State Study Commission for New York City to make a value judgment: to affirm that only if we trust the capacity of our mixed population to govern itself in the small areas as well as the large ones will our cities survive. This country's commitment to that proposition was made almost 200 years ago. Our City's survival requires that we reassert our confidence in its validity today.

What would be the effect of re-structure on Federal funds available to the City? Clearly, the answers to this query are of substantial importance to the Commission and to the citizens themselves.

We assigned the study of this question to Walter G. Farr, Jr., Professor of Law at New York University. We asked him to survey a representative sampling of Federal programs and to determine how they might operate under a re-structured government in which substantial budgetary and service-delivery powers would inhere in local governments within the City's boundaries.

The general conclusion is that Federal funding presents no substantial obstacle to effective re-structure of the City's government.

Task Force on Jurisdiction
and Structure

Edward N. Costikyan, Chairman

Maxwell Lehman, Vice Chairman

What effect would re-structuring the government of the City of New York have on the amount of Federal funds available for City programs? What other practical effects could decentralization have on Federally funded programs? Any evaluation of decentralization of responsibility for City services must consider whether Federal program rules could be adapted to a decentralized system.

Out of a total of $8.2 billion, the 1970-71 expense budget of the City of New York included some $1.3 billion of Federal funds.* The amount of Federal aid granted for the City's service programs has been increasing from year to year.

The conclusion, which we state at the outset, is that the Federal funding system presents no major obstacles to an effective program of re-structuring the City government.

SCOPE OF FEDERAL URBAN PROGRAMS
AND POSSIBLE FUTURE TRENDS

Over 75 percent of the Federal funds included in the City's 1970-71 expense budget consisted of direct or indirect payments to individuals for welfare and medical expenses. The City plays no role in selecting recipients of Medicaid and Medicare funds. It simply joins the State and Federal governments in reimbursing health professionals and health institutions that render services to eligible patients. While the City does process applications for welfare assistance to the aged and disabled and to families with dependent children, the proposed re-structure plan would not delegate this function to local district governments. Hence, decentralization would have no effect on the $1 billion of Federal Medicaid, Medicare, and categorical welfare funds.**

Of the remaining Federal funds, $117 million were Title I Elementary and Secondary Education Act (ESEA) grants, $65 million were Model Cities grants, and $44 million were poverty program grants. All of these grants are earmarked for areas of the City where needs are greatest, and all may be used to pay for a wide variety of activities. The City already successfully allocates ESEA funds to 31

---

*This amount does not include Federal funding of such State-administered programs as the Employment Service and Vocational Rehabilitation, nor Federal funds that are granted directly to private entities such as universities and voluntary hospitals.

**The Task Force has recommended that income maintenance be Federally funded, but that social services be locally delivered.

school districts, poverty program funds to 25 community corporations, and Model Cities funds to three model neighborhoods. Decentralization would not materially change this allocation process or the rules under which these Federal funds are used.

The balance of Federal funds available to the City are, for the most part, granted on a project-by-project basis. Except for urban renewal, most of these project grants are small in amount and are available only for narrowly defined uses. They are granted either for activities of limited duration or for the first few years of operation of pilot projects. New local district governments would be eligible to apply directly under most of these special programs. In other cases, the central City could be directly responsible to the Federal funding agency, as it is today. Indeed, the Human Resources Administration or Board of Education could be a vehicle for requesting grants for experimental and innovative purposes from Federal funding sources and apportioning those grants to various local districts. Even if local districts went directly to the funding source, the central agency staff could help prepare or review applications. It would not be particularly efficient to develop grantsmanship capacity in each of the proposed 30 or 35 local districts. The maximum possible amount of money going directly to a district would be small, since the total amount of Federal funds available for nonformula grants nation-wide is not large.*

While it is hazardous to predict the future course of Federal funding arrangements, it seems likely that forthcoming changes will tend to consolidate grants, lessen specific Federal program require-ments, favor general-purpose governmental units as grant recipients, and allocate funds on a geographic formula basis rather than a project-by-project basis.

For example, the Nixon administration has proposed combining urban renewal, public facilities, housing rehabilitation, and Model Cities grants into one flexible community development block grant to cities. The omnibus housing and urban development bill that passed the U.S. Senate keeps Model Cities separate, but does combine the other categorical programs into such a comprehensive community development grant program. This is a program that New York City could use partially to fund centrally controlled, large-scale renewal projects and partially to give local districts flexible funds for local physical improvement activities.

*But the local districts should be permitted to seek such grants, if they want to, and to develop the necessary grantsmanship techniques.

HOW SEVERAL TYPICAL FEDERAL PROGRAMS NOW
OPERATE AND HOW THEY MIGHT OPERATE
UNDER DECENTRALIZATION

Federal grant-in-aid arrangements for urban programs vary widely in terms of eligible sponsors, methods of allocating funds, and program requirements. Some programs are not available to city governments at all. Such programs as vocational rehabilitation and employment security are allocated on a formula basis to states and are administered directly by state agencies. Other programs involve grants made directly to such private institutions as universities and voluntary hospitals to help pay for research or experimentation.*

Health, Education, and Welfare Programs

Most programs of the U.S. Department of Health, Education, and Welfare (HEW), for which local governments are eligible sponsors, involve formula grants to state agencies, which then distribute them among local governments. Title I of the Elementary and Secondary Education Act (ESEA) is such a program. Other Federal programs assist local planning and coordinating efforts; the Comprehensive Health Planning Program is a typical one, involving both state and regional agencies. HEW also makes a number of grants for pilot or research programs and for continuing operation of such specialized programs as venereal disease control.

Grants Made under Title I of the
Elementary and Secondary Education Act

Under Title I of the Elementary and Secondary Education Act (1965), HEW grants more than $1 billion a year to state departments of education "to provide financial assistance to local education agencies serving areas with concentrations of children from low income families to expand and improve their educational programs . . . (to meet) the special educational needs of educationally deprived children."[8]

Funds are allocated to the states in accordance with a formula based primarily on the number of children either supported by the

---

*This appendix omits discussion of all such programs, because neither New York City nor any new local district government would have access to them.

Federally assisted program called Aid to Families with Dependent Children (AFDC) or from nonwelfare families with annual incomes of less than $2,000. HEW determines how much goes to the local education agencies in each county, on the basis of census and welfare data. The State makes allocations to individual education agencies outside New York City on the basis of poverty statistics and quality of project applications.

New York City is considered a local education agency and receives all the funds allocated to its five counties. The City's central Board of Education is expected to allocate these funds among the City's community school districts on a strict formula basis reflecting the number of children on the welfare rolls and children whose families have less than $2,000 in annual income but are not on welfare.*

Community school districts in the City can spend funds only for projects approved by the State. The City Board of Education is supposed to review project applications for form only, but the central board has tried to force the local community school boards to use Title I ESEA funds to pay for "More Effective Schools" projects, which the central board developed with the United Federation of Teachers (UFT) and which are referred to in the UFT's collective bargaining agreement. Last spring, the Supreme Court for New York County ruled that the City Board could not determine how community school boards use Title I ESEA funds, but the issue illustrates how centrally bargained labor agreements could restrict local flexibility regarding Federal funds.

Decentralization would not affect the amount of these Title I ESEA funds available to the City as a whole or the role of the Federal government.

As a practical matter, New York State now plays only a nominal role with respect to Title I ESEA funds for New York City. While the State has authority to disapprove applications for ESEA-funded projects, it has never exercised this power. Every project must contain an evaluation component, and the State reviews all evaluation reports. So far, the State has limited itself to guidance bulletins. If the community school boards or the proposed new local district governments became local education agencies and completely bypassed the City, the State may play a more assertive role. Within the counties,

---

*During the first several years, allocations among districts also reflected the central board's commitment to certain ongoing programs that the community school boards were required to continue. See memorandum, "Acting Superintendent to the Chairmen of Local School Boards," July 6, 1970.

the State has some flexibility on fund allocations, and it could devise
a somewhat different allocation formula for New York City's counties.
It could concentrate funds, for example, in districts with greater
poverty. The State could also become much more active in reviewing
project applications.

The role of the City would not have to change, though it might
make sense to eliminate the central Board's formal review of local
project applications. Many problems continue to plague school decentralization, particularly with respect to fiscal and personnel matters,
but these problems do not stem from Federal regulations or funding.
And any changes in the school decentralization law that may accompany
multi-purpose political decentralization would not create problems
with City-Federal relations.

Comprehensive Health Planning

Through national research institutes, grants for construction of
health facilities, support for control of communicable diseases, and
grants for a variety of experimental and pilot health care projects,
the Federal government has long been a major factor in the financing
of health research, disease prevention, and health care programs.
In addition, Medicare and Medicaid pay individual health care expenses
for the poor and the aged. But until recently, the Federal government
has not supported any geographically based comprehensive health
planning or service systems, because health care in the United States
is delivered primarily on a pluralistic market basis by private
practitioners and institutions.

The Federal government began to support comprehensive health
planning in the mid-1960s. Federally assisted state and regional
agencies analyze health needs and resources comprehensively on a
state-wide and regional basis, set priorities, and encourage public
and private agencies to adjust their activities to meet perceived needs
and priorities and to coordinate their activities. These planning
agencies also review and comment on applications for Federal assistance for health facility construction, for certain health training and
manpower programs, and for a newly authorized program of assistance
to prepaid group-practice health-maintenance organizations, designed
primarily to provide health services to residents of areas not adequately served by existing facilities.

While the bulk of Federal support for health care will probably
continue to go directly to individuals through an insurance scheme,
some supplementary governmental subsidy may well be needed for
health maintenance organizations to assure quality health care in
urban and rural poverty areas. Such subsidized health maintenance
organizations could presumably be public or private, but it seems

likely that they will be monitored by the new Comprehensive Health
Planning Agencies (CHPA). Such agencies may, therefore, play a
significant role in developing and monitoring the health care system
as it evolves in the next decade or so.

In New York City, the official CHPA is a division of the Health
Services Administration, although a majority of its governing board
represents consumers and a minority represents private health
providers. The CHPA recognized from the start that, because of the
City's size, complexity, and local variations, both detailed (operational)
planning and project reviews could best be accomplished by establishing
a network of district boards. The CHPA is presently working with
local groups to set boundaries for some 30 planning districts. The
central CHPA will presumably be responsible for City-wide or inter-
district health planning and project review, and the district boards
will be concerned with activities and facilities within their areas,
including most new health maintenance organizations.

The developing comprehensive health planning system would
appear to be fully compatible with the decentralization model developed
by this Task Force. Those health activities that could be decentralized
would be the responsibility of CHPA district boards, which would be
appointed either by the local councils or by the district executives.
Health planning districts could coincide with local government districts;
such an arrangement presents no difficulty. Indeed, the existence of
such a two-tier CHPA system should smooth the relations between a
partially decentralized City government and the Federal government
on all health matters.

Venereal Disease Control Programs

HEW administers several grant programs to help states and cities
control venereal disease (VD). Typically, the state or local government
develops, controls, staffs, and finances treatment facilities, and the
Federal government helps fund—and to a large extent staffs—VD
control efforts, including public education and tracking down contacts
of reported VD cases. Federal funds earmarked for VD control have
fallen off in recent years, but with attention focused on rising VD
rates, increased Federal funding seems likely.

In New York State, the State health authorities are largely responsible for processing applications for Federal funds for local programs
outside New York City. The City works directly with the Federal
government and is presently receiving about $1 million for VD control—
two-thirds going for costs of 55 Public Health Service officers assigned
to the City and one-third in cash for other program expenses. The
City employs another 50 City employees as VD control officers. The
control program works out of 13 VD clinics in the City, but all 105 VD

control officers are coordinated by a central office headed by a U.S.
Public Health Service officer, who in turn reports to the City official
in charge of the City-wide VD treatment and control program.

VD treatment activities could probably be decentralized to
district health departments, though there are economies of scale in
the 13 existing clinics. But VD treatment is not popular with physicians,
and VD clinics have no supportive constituency. Hence, there is the
danger that local districts would use flexible funds for more socially
acceptable health problems.

There is no reason why a VD clinic would be necessary in every
local district. The local authorities could contract with each other for
joint use of clinics. This is a decision to be made by health authorities
on the basis of relevant statistical data. But there is another view.
VD officials now can almost keep up with the City-wide tracing of VD
contacts and can coordinate a modest public education program. This
detection and public education work could not be carried on as efficiently on a district-by-district basis.

If the VD control program were decentralized, it is likely that
the State health authorities would assume greater control, as they are
authorized to do by Federal law. State surveillance could mean better
coordination of cases involving contacts across City lines, or it could
just mean another layer of bureaucracy. But if the one large VD
control program for the City as a whole were broken up into 30 or 40
smaller programs—comparable to the VD control programs in the
rest of the State—the State could well cut off the City's special direct
access to Federal funds and Federal officials.

Housing and Urban Development and Office of
Economic Opportunity Programs

The U.S. Department of Housing and Urban Development (HUD)
usually makes grants directly to cities on a project-by-project basis.
We will discuss two of that department's major programs, Urban
Renewal and Model Cities, together with one of its smaller programs,
Neighborhood Facilities. The Office of Economic Opportunity (OEO)
also makes grants directly to cities. We will suggest how the OEO's
Community Action Program could be adapted to a re-structured City.

Urban Renewal Programs

Federal grants for two-thirds of the cost of urban renewal projects have for years constituted a major source of capital for the City.
HUD makes grants on a project-by-project basis directly to the "local
public agency." In New York City, the "local public agency" is the
City itself.

The City used to receive about $60 million per year—about 6 percent of HUD's annual urban renewal funds. Recently, though, no such rule of thumb seems to have been in force, and the City's share now depends on the quality of its applications, the performance of the City on its existing renewal programs, and HUD's own priorities. The State contributes one-sixth of the costs of Federally assisted projects. While the State has review and approval power over the projects it assists, the State has as yet taken little substantive part in the City's urban renewal process.

In the City, the Housing and Development Administration (HDA) selects sites for renewal projects, which must have City Planning Commission and Board of Estimate approval. The HDA plans and executes renewal projects out of its downtown Manhattan office. Increasingly, however, in recent years, HDA has decentralized its day-to-day authority, devolving it to project directors, who, in turn, work with citizen project area committees. Planning authority should probably not be decentralized for large projects that involve substantial change in land use patterns. City-wide interests must generally take priority over local interests. Unpopular decisions could be taken more easily by a City-wide agency than they could by the local districts. But local districts must have a voice in decisions affecting them. Central government project directors should be given authority to work directly with local district governments, if those governments are established. For large projects, of City-wide significance, therefore, there would be no change in the Federal-City urban renewal relations.

Local district governments, however, could be given authority to apply directly to the Federal government for urban renewal grants for small projects, usually those involving rehabilitation of existing housing, small commercial developments, and related public facility improvements.

Authorization for such power by local districts could be accomplished by amendment of the State urban renewal legislation. Under the present State Urban Renewal Law, however, New York City's Charter determines which unit of City government shall be the "governing body" for purposes of approving most urban renewal activities. Local district governments, therefore, could probably be given sufficient authority in a new City Charter, without new State legislation. Whatever the source of authority for local district governments, there should be no legal difficulty with HUD, as Federal law simply indicates that grants and contracts should be made with authorized public bodies.

If the central City and the local districts were to have concurrent urban renewal authority, it might make sense to develop some system for rationing scarce Federal dollars among the possible City applicants.

The Housing and Development Administration or its successor agency, and the central Bureau of the Budget could determine the City's priorities, but it might be appropriate to require City Council approval if the councilmanic districts are coextensive with the local government districts. The council would then include the spokesmen of local district interests.

If a remodeled Board of Estimate—the proposed City Policy Board—were to play the role of referee between the central City and the districts, the Policy Board should pass on allocations of the City's annual urban renewal funds. Once the priority of a district project is set, the district government should be free to deal directly with HUD, so as to avoid layers of decisions and control. Alternatively, the central City and the local districts could compete for Federal dollars.

If the Federal administration's proposed comprehensive community development grant program becomes law, New York City could continue to use part of those funds for urban renewal activities under the State urban renewal statute. And some of those funds could be passed on to local districts under arrangements discussed above. Or the City could use those Federal funds either for community development programs centrally or for use by districts without regard to State urban renewal legislation. But in that case, the State urban renewal law should probably be amended to foreclose any claim that the State has preempted the field by its urban renewal legislation. In any event, as far as Federal rules are concerned, adoption by the Congress of the community development grant program would increase City flexibility.

Neighborhood Facilities

Under Section 703 of the Housing and Urban Development Act of 1965, HUD can make grants of up to two-thirds of the construction costs of a neighborhood multi-purpose service center to local public bodies authorized by State law to finance such a capital improvement. Limited Federal funds are awarded on a project-by-project basis. Priority is given to facilities in poor neighborhoods. The key to funding is the ability to pull together a comprehensive integrated system of needed health, welfare, recreational, cultural, and social services. The State plays no role in this program.

In New York City, the City itself is the neighborhood facilities grantee. The Housing and Development Administration handles site selection and construction, and a small office in the Human Resources Administration (HRA) is responsible for working with neighborhood organizations and with public and private agencies whose services are needed. In most cases, the City must put up much more than one-third of the construction costs, because the "fair" share of available Federal funds never covers the remaining two-thirds of the City's high construction costs.

New York City has moved slowly in carrying out multi-service center projects. A center cannot be properly designed until it is known what services the center will provide. Inexperienced representatives of poverty neighborhoods find it hard to develop a neighborhood consensus as to service priorities—and even harder to coordinate the component agencies of the City's Human Resources and Health Services Administrations, as well as private service agencies. The small coordinating office in HRA has not had enough power to force prompt commitments from City service agencies or City overhead agencies such as the Bureau of the Budget, the Personnel Department, and the Public Works Department. A neighborhood center is too small a project for sustained top level attention, and coordination below that level is almost impossible to achieve among City-wide agencies. As a result, the Hunts Point Multi-Service Center in the Bronx, begun as a high-priority showcase project in 1966, has not even been scheduled for occupancy until 1973.

Neighborhood center projects should be much easier to develop under decentralization. The State Legislature or a new City Charter might authorize the new district governments to qualify as legal entities, which could then finance capital improvements for services for which they were responsible. Subsequently, they could apply directly for Federal funding. Such district governments should be able to work more effectively with sponsoring neighborhood groups than under the present arrangements. District governments would also be responsible for most of the services these centers would deliver. If civil service rules were to allow local hiring, satisfactory staffing would also be easier to achieve. Persuading private agencies to give up some of their independence would still be difficult, but the local district governments would probably have power over some of the funding of most of such agencies. While New York City's share of the scarce Federal dollars would not increase, the local districts should be able to make much more effective use of the Neighborhood Facilities program.

Model Cities

HUD's Model Cities grants must be used to improve the quality of life in poor neighborhoods, and New York City's government must assure widespread citizen participation in program planning and implementation. Cities are supposed to concentrate on areas containing 10 percent of their populations. New York City has designated central Brooklyn, Harlem, and the south Bronx as Model Neighborhoods. Most cities, including New York, have developed elaborate neighborhood administrative structures with elected citizen boards. However, these structures have not stimulated widespread participation and have little political following or influence. The net result has been a series of useful projects, but little or no change in neighborhood or City-wide administrative or political arrangements.

If Model Cities funds continue to flow and if New York City creates new local district governments, the City's Model Neighborhood boundaries should be adjusted to conform to the new local district boundaries. Model Cities grants would then become, in effect, block grants to three or four of the neediest of the new districts. Hiring of neighborhood residents would conform perfectly to Federal guidelines for "enlarged opportunities for work" for neighborhood residents. The district council would probably qualify as a citizen participation structure, although some form of advisory committee with guaranteed membership from minority and poverty groups might be retained, at least for a while. Since the Model Cities program is supposed to be experimental and is aimed at achieving some of the same purposes as would be supported by decentralization, it seems likely that HUD would be receptive to such initiatives.

If the national administration's community development revenue-sharing grant program is passed, and if Model Cities becomes part of this comprehensive effort, the City could still allocate part of its share of the funds as block grants to these same districts. Or the City could cease preferring some poverty areas over others and spread these Federal funds more evenly among poorer districts throughout the City.

The Community Action Program

New York City's community corporations provide jobs for minority persons, practical education in politics and public administration, and rallying points for pressure on government from minority and poverty points of view. But the corporations are responsible for no significant governmental services and have had little impact on the performance of regular public or private service agencies. At least in theory, the new decentralized governments would fulfill the political objectives of the poverty programs at the same time that they take responsibility for delivering local services. Poverty program leaders should be in good positions to assume political leadership in new district governments, if they have, in fact, been representing majority community views. In theory, then, these scarce, flexible Federal funds should be transformed into block grants to the district governments in poverty areas, and the community corporations should be disbanded.

But the poverty bureaucracy would most certainly resist dismantling the community corporations. They would argue that the poor would not be guaranteed effective representation in many new district governments in which they would be a minority and that this one certain voice for the interests of the disadvantaged should not be stilled. If the community corporations continue their operations, the City should contribute only enough of its own funds to assure full Federal funding, and it should divert any savings to the new district governments. It should be mentioned here that the first report of the Task Force recommended local council election districts of 20,000 to 30,000 population. This should assure representation of all the diverse groups within a district. That report also recommended that community corporations be made accountable to the local councils.

Conclusion

Some State enabling legislation could have to be amended to authorize the new district governments to receive Federal funds as local public bodies, as sponsors of capital projects, or as units willing to create housing or renewal agencies; this would have resulted in the relevant State-wide laws being brought into line with the provisions of the proposed new City Charter. In other cases, Federal agencies could have to amend their regulations or procedures so that district governments can qualify as City demonstration agencies (Model Cities) or community action agencies. In a few cases, the City could be the Federal grantee, but it could delegate administrative responsibilities to the appropriate district government or governments.

Federal funding regulations present no substantial obstacle to effective decentralization of the City's government.

SUMMARY OF FINDINGS

1. Re-structuring the City government as proposed by the Task Force should have little or no effect on Federal funds available for programs within the City's borders.

2. Re-structuring would have no effect on the allocation of the billion dollars of Federal Medicaid, Medicare, and categorical welfare funds.

3. The City already distributes $117 million of Federal grants (Title I ESEA) among 31 school districts, along with poverty program funds among 25 community corporations and Model Cities funds among three neighborhoods. Decentralization would not materially alter the allocation process.

4. Any change in the school decentralization law that may accompany multipurpose political decentralization should not create problems with regard to City-Federal relationships.

5. The developing comprehensive health planning system would appear to be fully compatible with the decentralization design.

6. Federally-funded venereal disease treatment activities— selected as a typical program for purposes of discussion—could probably be decentralized to local district health departments, though there are economies of scale in the 13 existing clinics. The local authorities could contract with each other for joint use of clinics.

7. In urban renewal projects under the re-structuring plan proposed, local districts must have a voice in decisions affecting them. But City-wide interests should generally take priority over local interests. For large projects of City-wide significance, there-fore, there would be no change in the Federal-City urban renewal structure. Local governments, however, may be given authority to apply directly to the Federal government for urban renewal grants for small projects, usually those involving rehabilitation of existing housing, small commercial developments, and related local public facility improvements.

8. Whatever the source of authority for local district govern-ments, there should be no legal difficulty with the U.S. Department of Housing and Urban Development, as Federal law simply indicates that grants and contracts be made with authorized public bodies. The proposed City Policy Board (replacing the Board of Estimate) would pass on allocations of the City's annual urban renewal funds.

9. While New York City's share of neighborhood facilities funding would not increase, the proposed local districts ought to be able to make much more effective use of the Neighborhood Facilities program.

10. Model Neighborhood boundaries should be adjusted to conform to the new local district boundaries. Model Cities grants would then become, in effect, block grants to three or four of the neediest districts. Hiring of neighborhood residents would conform to Federal guidelines for "enlarged opportunities for work" for neighborhood residents.

11. Federal funding regulations present no substantial obstacle to effective re-structuring of the City's government.

1. Peter Eisinger, "Control-Sharing in the City: Some Thoughts on Decentralization and Client Representation" (paper delivered at the sixty-sixth annual meeting of the American Political Science Association, Los Angeles, September 8-10, 1970).

2. See William A. Robson and D. E. Regan, eds., Great Cities of the World: Their Government, Politics and Planning (London: George Allen and Unwin; Beverly Hills, Calif.: Sage Publications, 1972).

3. For a more complete discussion of criteria for allocation of services, see Performance of Urban Functions: Local and Areawide, U.S. Advisory Commission on Intergovernmental Relations (Washington, D.C., September 1963), Ch. 2, pp. 41-60.

5. Let There Be Commitment, Institute of Public Administration (1966).

6. Martin Tolchin, "The Budget Mystique," New York Times, May 24, 1972.

7. Reshaping Government in Metropolitan Areas, Committee for Economic Development (New York, 1970), p. 18.

8. Elementary and Secondary Education Act of 1965, 20 United States Code, 241(a) et seq.

RE-STRUCTURE AND CITIZEN INVOLVEMENT

Abrams, Robert. A Plan For Borough and Neighborhood Government
in New York City: A Proposal for Community Consideration.
New York: Office of the Bronx Borough President, October 1970.

Advisory Commission on Intergovernmental Relations. The New Grass
Roots Government? Decentralization and Citizen Participation
in Urban Areas. Washington, D.C., January 1972.

Altshuler, Alan A. Community Control: The Black Demand for Participation in Large American Cities. New York: Western
Publishing, 1970.

Association of the Bar of the City of New York. A Discussion Draft:
For a Symposium on Decentralizing New York City Government.
New York: the Association, 1970.

Bell, D., and V. Held. "The Community Revolution." Public Interest,
Summer 1969.

Benson, Charles S., and Peter B. Lund. Neighborhood Distribution of
Local Public Services. Berkeley, Calif.: Institute of Governmental Studies, University of California, 1969.

Bergsman, Joel. Alternatives to the Non-Gilded Ghetto: Notes on
Different Goals and Strategies: A Working Paper. Rev. ed.
Washington, D.C.: The Urban Institute, February 1970.

Berube, Maurice R. "The School Elections: Analysis and Interpre-
tation." Community (April 1970).

Black, Guy. The Decentralization of Urban Government: A Systems
Approach. Staff Discussion Paper 102, Program of Policy Studies
in Science and Technology. Washington, D.C.: George Washington University, August 1968.

Brower, Michael. The Criteria For Measuring the Success of a Community Corporation in the Ghetto. Cambridge, Mass.: Center
for Community Economic Development, 1970.

_____ . Why Do We Need Community Development Corporations for Ghetto Development? Cambridge, Mass.: Center for Community Economic Development, 1970.

Calambe, B. E. "Community Patrol: Los Angeles' Planned Police-Slumdweller 'Buffer' in Dispute." Wall Street Journal, August 2, 1967.

Callahan, John, and Donna E. Shalala. "Some Fiscal Dimensions of Three Hypothetical Decentralization Plans." Education and Urban Society, Vol. 2, November 1969.

Citizens for Local Democracy. How to Make the United States a Democracy. New York, 1970.

Citizens League. Sub-Urbs in the City. Minneapolis, Minn., 1970.

Citizens Union and Citizens Housing and Planning Council of New York City. A Program for Community Districts. New York, June 1964.

Clark, K. A Relevant War Against Poverty: A Study of Community Action and Social Change. New York: Harper and Row, 1969.

Committee for Economic Development. Modernizing Local Government. New York, 1966.

Conant, R. W. The Politics of Community Health. Washington, D.C.: Public Affairs Press, 1968.

Connorton, John V. Deputy Mayor-City Administrator—Unfinished Business. New York: Office of the City Administrator, 1965.

_____ . Office of the Mayor—Organizational Structure: Administrative Supervision of the Mayor's Agencies. New York: Office of the City Administrator, 1965.

Cunningham, L. L., and R. O. Nystrand. Citizen Participation in School Affairs. Washington, D.C.: Urban Coalition, 1969.

Dahl, Robert. "The City in the Future of Democracy." American Political Science Review, Vol. 61 (December 1967), pp. 953-72.

Demas, B. The School Elections: A Critique of the 1969 New York City School Decentralization. New York: Institute for Community Studies, 1971.

Educational Research Service. Decentralization and Community Involvement: A Status Report. Washington, D.C.: American Association of School Administrators, 1969.

Eisenger, P. "Central-Sharing of Administrative Functions in the City." (Presented at the Annual Meeting of the American Political Science Association, Los Angeles, 1970).

Fesler, J. "Approaches to the Understanding of Decentralization," in Governing the States and Localities, D. Lockard, ed., New York: Macmillan, 1969.

Frischknecht, R. L. "The Democratization of Administration: The Farmer Committee System." American Political Science Review, Vol. 47; September 1953, pp. 704-27.

Gittell, Marilyn. "New York City School Decentralization." Community, New York: Institute of Community Studies, Queens College, May 1969.

_____, and Maurice R. Berube. Confrontation at Ocean Hill-Brownsville. New York: Praeger Publishers, 1969.

Glazer, Nathan. "For White and Black, Community Control is the Issue." New York Times Magazine, April 27, 1969.

Glick, Brian. "Review; Institute for Policy Studies: Neighborhood Foundations Memoranda." Yale Law Journal, Vol. 76, May 1967, pp. 1258-72.

Goodpaster, Gary S. "An Introduction to the Community Development Corporation." Journal of Urban Law, Vol. 46, 1969, pp. 603-65.

Hallman, Howard W. "Guidelines for Neighborhood Management." Public Management, January 1971.

Hunter, Floyd. Community Power Structure—A Study of Decision Makers. New York: Anchor Books, 1963.

Joint Committee of the Citizens Union and Citizens Housing and Planning Council of New York City. A Program for Community Districts. June 1964.

Kahn, Alfred. Neighborhood Information Centers: A Study and Some Proposals. New York: Columbia University School of Social Work, 1966.

Kain, John F., and Joseph J. Persky. "Alternatives to the Gilded Ghetto." The Public Interest, Vol. 14, Winter 1969, pp. 74-87.

Kaufman, Herbert. "Administrative Decentralization and Political Power." Public Administration Review, Vol. 29, January/February 1969, pp. 3-15.

Krikus, R. "White Ethnic Neighborhoods—Ripe for the Bulldozer?" New York: American Jewish Committee, Middle America Pamphlet Series, 1970.

Kotler, Milton. Neighborhood Government: The Local Foundations of Political Life. Indianapolis and New York: Bobbs-Merrill, 1969.

_____. "The Radical Politics of Local Control." Christianity and Crisis, Vol. 29, June 9, 1966, pp. 160-62.

_____. "Two Essays on the Neighborhood Corporation." Urban America: Goals and Problems, Washington, D.C.: U.S. Congress, Joint Economic Committee, Subcommittee on Urban Affairs, 1967, pp. 170-91.

Kramer, R. M. Participation of the Poor. Englewood Cliffs, N. J.: Prentice Hall, 1969.

Kristol, Irving. "Decentralization for What?" Public Interest, Vol. 11, Spring 1968, pp. 17-25.

Leiserson, A. Administrative Regulation: A Study in Representation of Interests. Chicago: University of Chicago Press, 1942.

Leone, Sebastian. Proposed Plan For Local Government. New York: Office of the Brooklyn Borough President, February 24, 1972.

Levine, N. Ocean Hill-Brownsville, Schools in Crisis. New York: Popular, 1969.

Lindsay, John V. A Plan for Neighborhood Government for New York City. New York: Office of the Mayor, June 1970.

Lipsky, M. "Toward a Theory of Street-Level Bureaucracy." (Presented at the Annual Meeting of the American Political Science Association, New York, 1969).

Local Government in Greater London 1957-1960. Report presented to
    Parliament by Command of Her Majesty. London: Her Majesty's
    Stationery Office, October 1960.

Lopate, C., E. Flaxman, E.M. Bynum, and E.W. Gordon. "Decen-
    tralization and Community Participation in Public Education."
    Review of Educational Research, February 1970.

Mann, S. "Participation of the Poor and Model Cities in New York
    City." (Prepared for discussion at the National Academy of
    Public Administration, May 1970).

Miller, S.M., Martin Rein, and Mary Morgan. "The Future of Com-
    munity Participation." (Unpublished paper prepared for the
    Committee for Economic Development, May 28, 1969).

_____, and Martin Rein. "Participation, Poverty and Administra-
    tion." Public Administration Review, Vol. 29, January/Febru-
    ary 1969, pp. 15-25.

Moynihan, Daniel P. Maximum Feasible Misunderstanding: Community
    Action in the War on Poverty. New York: Free Press, 1969.

National Commission on Community Health Services. Health is a
    Community Affair. Cambridge, Massachusetts: Harvard
    University Press, 1966.

O'Donnell, Edward J. "The Neighborhood Service Center: Trends
    and Developments." Welfare in Review, January/February 1968.

Perry, Clarence A. "The Neighborhood Unit." Regional Survey of
    New York and Its Environs, Vol. VII, New York: Regional Plan
    Association, 1929.

Perry, Stewart E. A Note on the Genesis of the Community Develop-
    ment Corporation. Cambridge, Mass.: Center for Community
    Economic Development, 1970.

Public Administration Review. "Symposium on Alienation, Decen-
    tralization and Participation," Vol. 29, January/February 1969.

Rivera, Jose A. Community Development Corporations as Institutions
    for Social Innovation. Cambridge, Mass.: Center for Com-
    munity Economic Development, 1971.

Robin, Robert S. Private Enterprise and the Poor: Does A Partner-
    ship Make Sense? An Analysis of the Fiscal Aspects of the
    Community Self-Determination Act. 1969.

Robinson, Mariana. "Health Centers and Community Needs," in
    Governmental Reorganizations: Cases and Commentary,
    Frederick C. Mosher, ed., New York: Bobbs-Merrill, 1967.

Rosenbloom, Richard S., and Robin Marris. Social Innovation in the
    City: New Enterprises for Community Development, A Collec-
    tion of Working Papers. Harvard University Program on
    Technology and Society. Cambridge, Mass.: Harvard University
    Press, 1969.

_____. "Corporations for Urban Development," in Social Inno-
    vation in the City, Richard Rosenbloom and Robin Marris eds.,
    Cambridge, Mass.: Harvard University Press, 1969.

Shalala, Donna E. Neighborhood Governance: Issues and Proposals.
    New York: National Project on Ethnic America, 1971. (Con-
    tains an extensive bibliography on the subject of decentralization
    of government and citizen participation.)

_____. Neighborhood Governments: Rationale, Functions, Size
    and Governmental Framework. New York: Institute of Human
    Affairs, 1971.

Shepps, C. G., and D. L. Madison. Evaluation of Neighborhood Health
    Centers: A Plan for Implementation. Washington, D.C.: Office
    of Economic Opportunity, July 1967.

Silver, G. A. "What Has Been Learned About the Delivery of Health
    Care Services to the Ghetto," in Medicine in the Ghetto.
    New York: Appleton-Century-Crofts, 1969.

Smith, Bruce L. R., and George LaNoue, eds. "Urban Decentralization
    and Community Participation" (Special Issue). American
    Behavioral Scientist, Vol. 15, September/October 1971. Bruce
    L. R. Smith, "Introduction," pp. 3-14; Suzanne Farkas, "The
    Federal Role in Urban Decentralization," pp. 15-35; Peter K.
    Eisinger, "Control Sharing in the City," pp. 36-51; Gary T.
    Marx and Dane Archer, "Citizen Involvement in the Law
    Enforcement Process," pp. 52-72; George R. LaNoue and Bruce
    L. R. Smith, "Political Evolution of School Decentralization,"
    pp. 73-93; James W. David, "Decentralization, Citizen

Participation and Ghetto Health Care," pp. 94-107; Donald Haider, "The Political Economy of Decentralization," pp. 108-29.

Spiegel, Hans B. C., et al. Neighborhood Power and Control: Implications for Urban Planning. New York: Institute of Urban Environment, School of Architecture, Columbia University, 1968.

Sterzer, Earl E. "Neighborhood Grant Program Lets Citizens Decide." Public Management (January 1971).

Sutton, Percy E. A Plan for Localized Government for New York City. New York: Office of the Manhattan Borough President, February 1972.

Task Force Report on Organization of Community Health Services. Health Administration and Organization in the Decade Ahead. Washington, D.C.: Public Affairs Press, 1967.

The George Gallup Organization, Inc. survey conducted for The Temporary State Commission to Make a Study of the Governmental Operation of the City of New York. "Attitudes of New Yorkers About Reorganizing Their City Government." New York, June 1, 1972.

"The Inner-City Development Corporation." Virginia Law Review, Vol. 55, June 1969, pp. 872-908.

Tobier, Arthur. "Cooperative Communities North and South: A Response to Poverty." The Urban Review, Vol. 2, April 1968, pp. 15-17.

United States Department of Housing and Urban Development. "Citizen Participation." CDA Letter 3, MCGR 3100.3, November 30, 1967.

Urich, Heidi. Community Development Corporations in Urban Settings: Twenty Case Studies. Cambridge, Mass.: Center for Economic Development, 1970.

Vietorisz, Thomas, and Bennett Harrison. The Economic Development of Harlem. New York: Praeger Publishers, 1970.

_____, and Bennett Harrison. "The Potential of Ghetto Development." (Paper prepared for the 1971 Northeastern Meetings of the Regional Science Association, Binghamton, N.Y., March 19-21, 1971).

Washnis, George J. Neighborhood Facilities and Municipal Decentralization. Vols. I and II. Washington, D.C.: Center for Governmental Studies, March 1971.

_____. Little City Halls. Washington, D.C.: Center for Governmental Studies, January 1971.

Waskow, A. I. Community Control of the Police. Institute for Policy Studies, Center for Emergency Support, Washington, D.C.: (mimeographed), N.d.

Wilson, J. Q. "The Urban Unease: Community vs. the City." Public Interest, Summer 1968, pp. 25-39.

Wilson, Kenneth D. "Neighborhood Proposal Aimed at Citizen Participation." Public Management, January 1971.

Zimmerman, Joseph F. "Heading Off City Hall—Neighborhood Wars." Nation's Cities, November 1970.

Zwieback, Burton. "Democratic Theory and Community Control." Community Issues, March 1969.

INTERGOVERNMENTAL RELATIONS

Adrian, C. "Governing Megacentropolis: The Politics." Public Administration Review, Vol. 70, September 1970, pp. 497-505.

Advisory Commission on Intergovernmental Relations. Multistate Regionalism. Washington, D.C., April 1972.

_____. Eleventh Annual Report. Washington, D.C., 1970.

_____. Fiscal Balance in the American Federal System. Vol. 1, Washington, D.C., 1967.

_____. Performance of Urban Function: Local and Areawide. Washington, D.C., 1963.

Aron, Joan B. The Quest for Regional Cooperation: A Study of the New York Metropolitan Regional Council. Berkeley, Calif.: University of California Press, 1969.

Banfield, E. "Revenue Sharing in Theory and Practice." Public
    Interest, Spring 1971.

Birsh, R. The Public Economy of Metropolitan Areas. Chicago:
    Markham, 1971.

Bollens, J. Special District Governments in the United States.
    Berkeley, Calif.: University of California Press, 1957.

Bollens, John C., and Henry J. Schmandt. The Metropolis: Its People,
    Politics, and Economic Life. New York: Harper and Row, 1965.

Campbell, Alan K., ed. The States and the Urban Crisis. Englewood
    Cliffs, N.J.: Prentice-Hall, 1970.

Chatters, Carl H., et al. Financing Metropolitan Government—A
    Symposium. Princeton, N.J.: Tax Institute, 1955.

Committee for Economic Development, Research and Policy Com-
    mittee. Reshaping Government in Metropolitan Areas. New
    York, February 1970.

Coulter, Philip B. Politics of Metropolitan Areas: Selected Readings.
    New York: Thomas Y. Crowell, 1967.

Derthick, M. The Influence of Federal Grants; Public Assistance in
    Massachusetts. Cambridge, Mass.: Harvard University Press,
    1970.

Duncan, Otis Dudley, et al. Metropolis and Region. Baltimore, Md.:
    The Johns Hopkins University Press, 1960.

Elazar, D. American Federalism: A View from the States. New
    York: Thomas Y. Crowell, 1966.

Eldredge, H. Wentworth, ed. Taming Megalopolis. Vols. I and II,
    Garden City, N.Y.: Anchor Books, 1967.

Erie, Steven P., et al. Reform of Metropolitan Governments. Balti-
    more, Md.: The Johns Hopkins University Press, 1972. (Booklet
    No. 1 in Resources for the Future series, The Governance of
    Metropolitan Regions, Lowdon Wingo, ed.)

Gottman, Jean. Megalopolis: The Urbanized Northeastern Seaboard
    of the United States. Norwood, Mass.: The Plimpton Press,
    1961.

Grant, D. "Urban Needs and State Response: Local Government
    Reorganization." The States and the Urban Crisis, Alan K.
    Campbell, ed., Englewood Cliffs, N.J.: Prentice-Hall, 1970.

Gulick, Luther Halsey. The Metropolitan Problem and American
    Ideas. New York: Alfred A. Knopf, 1962.

Hadden, Jeffrey K., Louis H. Masotti, and Calvin J. Larson, eds.
    Metropolis in Crisis: Social and Political Perspectives.
    Itasca, Ill.: F. E. Peacock Publishers, 1971.

Hoover, Edgar M., and Raymond M. Vernon. Anatomy of a Metropolis.
    Cambridge, Mass.: Harvard University Press, 1959.

Kaplan, Harold. Urban Political Systems, A Functional Analysis of
    Metropolitan Toronto. New York: Columbia University Press,
    1967.

Maass, A., ed. Area and Power, A Theory of Local Government.
    Glencoe, Ill.: Free Press, 1959.

Marshall, Dale Rogers, Bernard Frieden and Daniel W. Fessler.
    Minority Perspectives. Baltimore, Md.: The Johns Hopkins
    University Press, 1972. (Booklet No. 2 in Resources for the
    Future series, The Governance of Metropolitan Regions,
    Lowdon Wingo, ed.)

Metropolitan Fund, Inc. Regional Governance, A Dialogue Proceedings
    of a Seminar on "Reshaping Government in Metropolitan Areas."
    Detroit, January 1971. (This is a follow-up of the Committee
    for Economic Development report on Reshaping Government in
    Metropolitan Areas.)

Mogulof, Melvin B. Governing Metropolitan Areas. Washington, D.C.:
    The Urban Institute, December 1971.

New York State Joint Legislative Committee on Metropolitan and
    Regional Areas. Governing Urban Areas: Strengthening Local
    Government through Regionalism, 1968.

Office of Economic Opportunity. Catalogue of Federal Domestic
    Assistance. Washington, D.C., 1970, 1967.

Segal, M., and A. Fritschler. "Policy Making in the Intergovernmental
    System: Emerging Patterns and a Typology of Relationships."

(Presented at the Annual Meeting of the American Political
Science Association, Los Angeles, 1970).

Smith, Robert Gillian. Public Authorities in Urban Areas. Washington,
D.C.: National Association of Counties Research Foundation,
1969.

Sundquist, J., and D. Davis. Making Federalism Work. Washington,
D.C.: Brookings Institution, 1969.

The Government of Ontario. Design for Development: The Toronto-
Centered Region. May 1970.

Torres, Juan de. Government Services in Major Metropolitan Areas;
Functions, Costs, Efficiency. New York: The Conference
Board, 1972.

Verman, Raymond, Director. New York Metropolitan Region Study.
Graduate School of Public Administration of Harvard Univer-
sity, for the Regional Plan Association. Cambridge, Mass.:
Harvard University Press, 1960.

Vernon, Raymond. Metropolis—1985. Cambridge, Mass.: Harvard
University Press, 1960.

Watson, W. B., E. A. T. Barth, and D. P. Hayes. "Metropolitan
Decentralization through Incorporation." Western Political
Quarterly, Vol. 18, March 1965, pp. 198-206.

Weiler, Conrad J., Jr. "Metropolitan Federation Reconsidered."
Urban Affairs Quarterly, June 1971.

Wofford, John G., et al. Metropolitanization and Public Services.
Baltimore, Md.: The Johns Hopkins University Press, 1972.
(Booklet No. 3 in Resources for the Future series, The Govern-
ance of Metropolitan Regions, Lowdon Wingo, ed.)

Wood, Robert Caldwell. 1400 Governments (The Political Economy
of the New York Metropolitan Region). Cambridge, Mass.:
Harvard University Press, 1961.

Wright, D. Federal Grants-in-Aid. Washington, D.C.: American
Enterprise Institute, 1968.

SOURCE DOCUMENTS

Administrative Code of the City of New York. Six volumes. Albany:
    Williams Press, 1971.

Ash, Mark, and William Ash, eds. The Greater New York Charters
    as Enacted in 1897 and Amended in 1901. New York: Baker
    Voorhis, 1901. (The charter under which the City was governed,
    1902-37.)

Berman, Frederick S. "The New York City Charter—Some Important
Effects." New York Law Journal, January 25, 1963. editorial
    page.

Birdseye, Clarence F. The Greater New York Charter, Constituting
    Chapter 387 of the Laws of 1897. New York: Baker Voorhis,
    1897. (The report of the committee which drafted the charter
    and the report of the full Charter Commission to the legislature
    are included.)

Citizens Union. "How Ripper Charter Rips." The Searchlight, Vol. 1,
    August 9, 1911. (This special charter number presents the
    Citizens Union view of the City charter proposed that year.)

City Club of New York. The So-Called Gaynor Charter: What It Is
    and What It Does. New York: The City Club, 1911. (An un-
    favorable analysis of a proposed and eventually rejected
    charter.)

Forbes, Russell. "Charter Reform in New York City." National
    Municipal Review, Vol. 21, April 1932, pp. 168-71. (Explains
    the need for redesigning the City's government.)

Goodnow, Frank J. "The Charter of the City of New York." Political
    Science Quarterly, Vol. 17, 1902, pp. 1-23. (An expert analysis
    of the City's original charter that went into effect in 1898, and
    of the changes introduced by the charter of 1902.)

Institute of Public Administration. Governmental Organization within
    the City of New York. New York, 1949.

Mayor's Task Force on Reorganization of the New York City Govern-
    ment. Report and Proposed Local Law. New York: Office of
    the Mayor, 1966.

McGoldrick, Joseph D. "Is the City Manager Plan Suitable for New York?" National Municipal Review, Vol. 21, May 1932, pp. 289-92. (This article foreshadowed the rejection of the city-manager plan by the Thacher Charter Commission, of which McGoldrick was a member.)

New York City Charter Revision Commission. New York City Charter. Effective January 1, 1963, as amended to January 1969. New York: The City Record, 1963.

_____. Records of Public Hearings and Minutes of Executive Meetings, February 18, 1935-August 4, 1936. Four volumes, Kent Hall, Columbia University. (The papers and documents of the Thacher Commission, prepared by its counsel.)

_____, Summary. "A Guide to Important Changes Proposed Between the Old and New Charters," 1961, 4 pages.

"Proposals for the Reorganization of the City of New York." American Political Science Review, Vol. 27, April 1933, pp. 336-40. (Summarizes a spate of recommendations for charter revision, following the Seabury report.)

Pryor, James W. "The Greater New York Charter." Annals of the Academy of Political and Social Science, Vol. 10, 1897, pp. 23-28, 32. (An authoritative description of the first charter of the Greater City.)

Rowland, Howard S. The New York Times Guide to Federal Aid for Cities and Towns. New York: Quadrangle Books, 1971.

Savona, Francis, ed. Amendments to the Eagle Library Edition of the Charter of the City of New York from May 1, 1930 to the Close of the Extraordinary Sessions of the 1934 State Legislature. Brooklyn, New York: Brooklyn Eagle Library, 1934. (The versions of the charter employed by the Thacher Charter Commission.)

Shaw, Frederick. History of the New York City Legislature. New York: Columbia University Press, 1954. (Contains notes on charter commissions and proposals.)

Smith, Thelma. Guide to the Municipal Government of the City of New York. New York: Record Press, 1959, 1966. (1971 version, which will be published this year, contains many bibliographical references.)

Tanzer, Lawrence A. "The Defeat of the Tammany-Gaynor Charter."
    National Municipal Review, Vol. 1, January 1912, pp. 61-68.

_____. The New York City Charter Adopted November 3, 1936.
    New York: Clark Boardman, 1937. (The charter that went into
    effect in 1938, published by the associate counsel to the Charter
    Commission.)

Thacher, Thomas D. "Notes on the Work of the New York City Charter
    Revision Commission, Appointed 1936." Columbia University
    Oral History Collection, Special Collections, Butler Library
    (microfilm). (These papers and documents tell part of the
    story of the commission that drafted a home-rule charter.)

The Temporary State Commission to Make a Study of the Govern-
    mental Operations of the City of New York. New York City in
    Transition (1960 Interim Report). Ch. 2: "The Development of
    New York City's Governmental Structure: 1898 to the Present
    Charter," pp. 85-96; Ch. 3: "Recent Studies 1950-1956," pp.
    97-115 (this chapter provides a useful 12-page summary of the
    pre-1961 charter era).

Viertel, William, ed. New York City Charter Adopted at the General
    Election Held November 3, 1936. New York: City Record, 1958.
    (Issued periodically by this official source, this document is an
    authoritative text of the City charter, with amendments passed
    by local legislation and State law up to the date of publication.)

POLITICAL SCIENCE DOCUMENTS

Adrian, Charles R. Governing Urban America. New York: McGraw-
    Hill, 1961.

Advisory Commission on Intergovernmental Relations. "Neighborhood
    Sub-units of Government." State Legislative Program, Wash-
    ington, D.C., 1970.

Bacon, Edmund N., et al. "The Conscience of the City." Daedalus,
    Journal of the American Academy of Arts and Sciences,
    Stephen R. Graubard, ed., Richmond, Virginia: American
    Academy of Arts and Sciences, Fall 1968.

Banfield, E., and J. Wilson. City Politics. New York: Alfred A.
    Knopf, 1963.

_____. The Unheavenly City. Boston: Little, Brown, 1970.

Buchanan, J., and G. Tullock. The Calculus of Dissent. Ann Arbor,
    Mich.: University of Michigan Press, 1962.

Connery, Robert H., and Demetrios Coraley. Governing the City:
    Challenges and Options for New York. New York: Praeger
    Publishers, 1969.

Deutsch, Karl Wolfgang. The Nerves of Government: Models of
    Political Communication and Control. New York: The Free
    Press of Glencoe, 1963.

Fitch, Lyle C., and Annmarie Hauck Walsh, eds. Agenda for a City
    (Issues Confronting New York). Beverly Hills, Calif.: Sage
    Publications, 1970.

Greer, S. Urban Renewal and American Cities. New York: Bobbs-
    Merrill, 1965.

Hall, Peter. The World Cities. New York: McGraw-Hill Company,
    1966.

Lineberry, R., and F. Fowler "Reformism and Public Policies in
    American Cities," in City Politics and Public Policy, J. Q.
    Wilson, ed, New York: John Wiley, 1968, pp. 97-123.

Moynihan, Daniel P. "Toward a National Urban Policy." The Public
    Interest, Vol. 17, Fall 1969.

Pusic, Eugen, and Annmarie Hauck Walsh. Urban Government for
    Zagreb, Yugoslavia. New York: Praeger, Publishers, 1968.

Robson, William A., and D. E. Regan, eds. Great Cities of the World.
    Vols. I and II. Beverly Hills, Calif.: Sage Publications, 1972.

Sayre, Wallace S., and Herbert Kaufman. Governing New York City.
    New York: Norton and Company, 1965. (Contains numerous
    bibliographical references including a section on City charter
    documents and commentaries.)

Shank, Alan, ed. Political Power and the Urban Crisis. Boston:
    Holbrook Press, 1969.

Stanley, David T. Professional Personnel for the City of New York.
    Washington, D.C.: The Brookings Institution, 1963.

State of New York Temporary Commission on the Powers of Local Government. Interim Report. New York, 1972.

The Mayor's Commission on Management Survey. Modern Management for the City of New York. Vols. I and II. New York, March 30, 1953.

Walsh, Annmarie Hauck. The Urban Challenge to Government (An International Comparison of Thirteen Cities). New York: Praeger Publishers, 1969.

_____. Urban Government for the Paris Region. New York: Praeger Publishers, 1968.

Williams, Babatunde A., and Annmarie Hauck Walsh. Urban Government for Metropolitan Lagos. New York: Praeger Publishers, 1968.

EDWARD N. COSTIKYAN, an attorney, has been active in the fields of law and politics for many years. He graduated first in his class from Columbia Law School and served as law secretary to United States Judge Harold R. Medina. He then became an associate at the firm of Paul, Weiss, Rifkind, Wharton & Garrison, becoming a partner in the year 1960. He is a fellow of the American College of Trial Lawyers.

While pursuing his legal career, he also became active in Reform politics in New York City. He served from 1955 to 1965 as Democratic district leader in the 8th Assembly District South in Manhattan. Succeeding Carmine DeSapio, he became county leader of the Democratic County Committee of New York County in 1962 and served until the end of 1964.

In 1965, he was campaign manager for the Abraham Beame mayoralty ticket in the primary and general elections. In 1968, he was active in the Eugene McCarthy presidential campaign.

His book, Behind Closed Doors: Politics in the Public Interest, is widely used in college government courses. He has also written a number of articles on city government and on New York City government in particular.

In 1971, he was named chairman of the Task Force on Jurisdiction and Structure of the State Study Commission for New York City. The Task Force was charged with looking toward a re-structuring of New York City's government. This book consists of the Task Force's report.

MAXWELL LEHMAN, vice chairman of the Task Force on Jurisdiction and Structure, has been actively engaged in governmental and academic activities. Formerly City Administrator of the City of New York, he has also been Director of the Public Administration Center at Long Island University and Professor of Public Administration at New York University. He is now a member of the faculty at Fairfield University, teaching courses in political and managerial communication. He is also President of the Greater New York Study Group, Inc., a nonprofit governmental research corporation.

While with the City government, he was chairman of the Mayor's Emergency Control Board, chairman of the City-State Relations Committee, secretary of the Mayor's Cabinet, and a member of the New York City charter revision group named in 1960.

Professor Lehman helped create, and for ten years served as executive secretary of, the Metropolitan Regional Council, the organization of local governments in the New York-New Jersey-Connecticut metropolitan area. He was also public administration specialist for the Ford Foundation, serving for two years in North Africa. He has lectured to governmental and university groups in Europe on urban problems, transportation, and innovative approaches to city governance. For the United States Conference of Mayors, he prepared a study on the impact of Federal poverty programs upon local governments.

His education was at Rutgers University, New York University, and Harvard University.